In Search of Restoration and Eighteenth-Century Theatrical Biography

Papers Read at a Clark Library Seminar,
January 25, 1975

by

George Winchester Stone, Jr.
Philip H. Highfill, Jr.

WILLIAM ANDREWS CLARK
MEMORIAL LIBRARY
University of California, Los Angeles/1976

Introduction

Wᴇ ᴋɴᴏᴡ what interests us about the private and professional lives of actors and actresses, about green-room gossip and state performances. Ever since Plato banished actors from his ideal republic, many have shared his suspicion that role-playing has debilitating consequences, that the actor's flexibility denies moral stability to the man. Pope, it seems, might as well have written "most actors have no characters at all." Expecting their lives to be flamboyant, we dismiss as untypical those occasional records of long-lasting, staid monogamy in order to reflect, say, upon Mr. Richard Burton's interesting proposition that acting is best left to women, homosexuals, and persons of low intelligence. Actors, after all, ought to have interesting lives. Social intercourse has inescapably histrionic elements, and who better to perform socially than those trained to perform professionally? Their stage performances interest us for a more elevated reason. Performances interpret plays, and the history of performances belongs, in part, to the history of interpretations. Early records often tease us by their patchiness, but enough sometimes remains for us to reconstruct the interpretation of roles, if not whole productions.

George Winchester Stone, Jr., Dean and Professor of English, Emeritus, New York University, and Philip H. Highfill, Jr., Professor of English, The George Washington University, give us some sense in the following pages of just how much remains, how much delights, instructs, or teases by inconclusiveness. Both report on collaborative enterprises still in progress, Dean Stone describing a joint biography of Garrick, Professor Highfill the ambitious multi-volume dictionary of theatrical personnel between 1660 and 1800 which has occupied him and two others for more than twenty years. Professor Highfill scans a sea like that in Wordsworth's sonnet, "sprinkled far and nigh" with ships, some gallantly rigged, others barely marked. Dean Stone pursues with "lover's look" one "goodly vessel . . . come like a giant from a haven broad." Both are and have been much concerned with the problems and interests sketched above.

Players, at least the successful ones, are thought to be flamboyant, dissolute, even if they are not. Lionization walks a bare step before legend, and legend, the question of anecdote that occupies Professor Highfill, raises problems of evidence, its admissibility, inadmissibility. Professor Highfill counsels a proper scepticism, while Dean Stone finds Garrick to be not only among the half dozen great actors of the London stage, of highest importance in the history of interpretations, but also a gentleman quite undeserving the Socratic reproof. Both address themselves to questions of exclusion and inclusion from records sometimes scanty, sometimes too full. But both accept, as all must, that we are indebted to the players for making our lives less dull at times. We owe much to players, and not least of our obligations is to speak of them without dullness. The pages that follow show how thoroughly Dean Stone and Professor Highfill have discharged that obligation.

ALAN ROPER
University of California
Los Angeles

I

David Garrick and
the Eighteenth-Century Stage:
Notes toward a New Biography

GEORGE WINCHESTER STONE, JR.

In the 1930s, Jean Giraudoux wrote a play—*Amphytrion 38*—indicating, as all know, that his was the thirty-eighth composition on that engaging myth of celestial seduction. George M. Kahrl and I are now collaborating on what might be called *David Garrick 14,* since ours will be the fourteenth treatment of the life of that marvelous English actor, playwright, and theatre manager who raised the character of acting to the status of a liberal art, who displayed a genius for theatre administration unknown up to that time (and seldom since), who was an extraordinarily successful playwright and versifier whose death, as Dr. Johnson remarked, eclipsed the gaiety of nations. Garrick was also the embodiment of the best in an eighteenth-century gentleman—socially, morally, and personally.

Examination of the previous biographies reveals a pattern of repetitiveness and focus, somewhat askew—anecdotal in the extreme, mingling fact with fiction, and showing the man bouncing off the surface of eighteenth-century social life, making the rounds of the elite, lionized in society at home and abroad, vilified by authors whose plays he rejected and by rival actors, jealous of his reputation, careful of his money, tyrannical as a manager, brilliant as an actor, frothy as a playwright, engaging as a letter-writer and conversationalist —the antithesis of Dr. Johnson, the foil for Goldsmith, and the target for Horace Walpole.[1]

Support for the research herein has recently come from a generous grant from the National Endowment for the Humanities.

3

All this is pleasant, makes good reading, and much of it is true. Why go on, especially when the last three biographies have all been done, not a generation apart, but within the last twenty-five years, and all by women: Margaret Barton (1949), Anna Byrd Stewart (1952), and Carola Oman, Lady Lenanton (1958)? The first of these was popular but thin, the second a children's book, and the third the product of one trained as an historian, yet who dealt with but half the evidence. These three and the previous biographers, from Thomas Davies and Arthur Murphy (Garrick's contemporaries) to their nineteenth- and twentieth-century followers, James Boaden, Percy Fitzgerald, Joseph Knight, Mrs. Clement Parsons, and F. A. Hedgcock, were all charmed by the magnetism of the Garrick personality, all did well for their times and in view of the limited materials they had to work with. Some had biases which have persisted in the Garrick lore but which facts now known contradict.

But why go on indeed? "To exact of everyman who writes that he should say something new," wrote Dr. Johnson (*Idler* No. 85), "would be to reduce authors to a small number. . . . Yet surely there ought to be some bounds to repetition. Libraries ought no more to be heaped forever with the same thoughts differently expressed, than with the same books differently decorated." Distinctions, differences, newness count. What mainly prompts our new biography is the availability of abundant material hitherto unstudied. In the face of it former biases should fade.

The largest single Garrick collection in the world is in the Folger Shakespeare Library, opened in 1932, yet none of the last three biographers has visited that library for a studious session. And the great private libraries, such as the Folger and the William Andrews Clark and Huntington collections, cannot be bypassed by the serious scholar. Of the earlier biographers, Davies sought, but not very hard, to counteract the impression, saddled upon the actor by contemporary detractors, that Garrick was over-vain as an actor, avaricious and mean as a manager. Murphy destroyed the Davies defense by noting that Garrick, though a fine actor, was small-minded and tight-fisted off-stage. He perpetuated the thought that Garrick feared criticism, was wary of the waspish Samuel Foote, and manipulated the current press to his own best interests. Our study reveals Garrick in a new perspective, both as the most professional, in the fullest sense of the word, man of the theatre and as a most cultivated man of extensive individual and social interests.

He was as vain as any successful person, especially an actor, might be, and with eminently justifiable grounds. He loved a lord, and enjoyed participating in the conversation at table with the brightest and the best. But he was generous to both friend and foe. He wrote more letters of recommendation for friends and children of friends for jobs (and successfully too) than most college professors now do for their students. He recognized talent lurking under the crust of alcoholism, bailing Thomas Weston, the low comedian, out of jail time and again, and talent residing in the extremely provoking off-stage attitudes of Frances Abington. He loaned money to Laurence Sterne for his travels. His letter to the Marquis of Rockingham saved the life of fellow actor Turbot's son who had been accused of stealing a silver goblet.

Those who have visited that remarkable collection of human artifacts in the Sir John Soane Museum in London will have seen Hogarth's four wonderful paintings "The Election," brimming with London life and subtle in their satire. Those paintings long hung on Garrick's walls. How and why? A clipping in the Forster Collection in the Victoria and Albert Museum tells the story, and reveals the basic impulses toward generosity that animated David Garrick off stage. Hogarth told Garrick that he had finished the four, but would probably not find a buyer for the £ 200 he wanted for them, so would auction them off. He hoped Garrick would be among the bidders. Garrick thought it over and put up £ 10. Next day, says the clipping, he went out of his house and broke into the following soliloquy, as Mrs. Garrick related it: "What have I been doing? I have just put my name down for a few guineas at Mr. Hogarth's request, and as his friend, but now he must go to another friend, and then to another: to how many must he apply before he gets a sufficient number? This is mere begging; and should such a man as Hogarth be suffered to beg? Am not I his friend?" The result was that he instantly turned back, and purchased those fine pictures at the price of the 200 guineas which the artist himself had fixed.[2]

But Garrick's prudent management of the large and distinguished theatrical company at Drury Lane, and all of its fifty house servants, weighed even more in the scales of Garrick's human concern than his many exercises of generous impulse to individuals. He cared for the well-being of Drury Lane. He realized that the lives, hopes, and families of eighty to ninety persons depended upon the successful operation of that theatre. It must not fail (as it had often in the past). It must excel. He carried it through two major riots, wherein its benches were torn up and chandeliers broken. Nine times he refurbished it, rearranged its interior and exterior. Even upon the eve of his retiring he engaged the Adam brothers, architects of grace and beauty, to redo it inside, and reface its exterior, sinking £4,000 into a venture he was soon to leave. Over a thousand people gained a living and some security from his prudent and professional management.

One needs but read the pages of the *London Chronicle, St. James's Chronicle,* and the *Public Advertiser* for the long hot summer of 1772, and earlier ones for the year 1762, to witness the virulence of Grub-Street attacks on Garrick as a manager —almost all items coming from disappointed authors—and at the same time read his letters for those years to see that he feared no criticism, toadied to no pressures, even from a William Kenrick whose libelous attack darkly hinting a homosexual relationship between Garrick and the unfortunate Isaac Bickerstaffe was finally nullified by Kenrick's public retraction and apology. Garrick disliked carrying controversy to the public press, and specified in his understandings about joint management with James Lacy that neither upon misunderstandings should "vent any speeches in public," but both should settle matters by arbitration (Kahrl, III, p. 1350).

Garrick himself had recourse to the public press in his own defense only once, early in his career. He with Charles Macklin had led a boycott of Fleetwood's Drury Lane. Together with eight or nine other actors, they protested Fleetwood's management. They negotiated; Fleetwood would take all of them back *except* Macklin. They held out as long as they could. Garrick returned with the eight (who were practically starving) to the distress of Macklin. Macklin scurrilously attacked him in the public press, and Garrick then replied.[3] But under the battery of press comments throughout his career his letters, now fully documented, especially in response to later public attack, are calm, objective, and patient, exemplary in the handling of public relations and exemplary in the kind of professionalism his management stood for. That he had *no* manipulative influence over the press, we can now amply demonstrate for the first time since the imputation of meddling was made by the rejected author Thaddeus Fitzpatrick in 1762. Examination of his ownership of shares, limitations on the voting rights of shareholders, and his correspondence with publishers, combined with instances of their objective treatment of *all* contributors, constitute the evidence.

We are all familiar with the rule of thumb we customarily give students about English drama in the three centuries preceding ours. Namely, that the seventeenth century was the great age of creative drama (Shakespeare, Jonson, *et al.*); that the eighteenth was the age of great acting with its Bettertons, Cibbers, Macklins, Quins, and Garricks and half a dozen remarkable actresses, while the nineteenth century was the great age for the application of new technology to theatrical production—innovations with gas and electric lighting, the box set, detailed and historically accurate costuming, and the like. Recently interest has been renewed in and attention has increased about the vitality of the eighteenth-century theatre —its actors, its plays, its shifts in acting styles, its changes in theatre architecture, and its relation to the sister arts—and such interest has shifted from attention paid to "personalities" to concentration on professional qualifications for acting and management. Who was the one significant person at the center of this activity? David Garrick, of course. Without Garrick what would have been the course of eighteenth-century theatre and drama? This actor, manager, playwright was so vital to the development of the stage and the art of drama that had he not been there dramatic production would have existed in a really ho hum atmosphere. Yet, *with* him the London stage became the glory of the nation and the envy of all European culture.

Materials and total evidence are at last at hand for a thorough and startling biography of a genius who has left his impact to this day. The memory of Betterton has dimmed. Colley Cibber, amusing but mostly for his own "Apology" for his life, has long been forgotten. Fat and stolid James Quin declaimed well in his time but became outmoded even before his death. The fierce and litigious Charles Macklin carried on, but pathetically, well into his nineties. But Garrick, brimming with ideas, aware that he could carry them out best if he were also in management's chair, set professional standards for his whole company, exemplified them himself, commissioned the best among contemporary musical composers, employed the finest dancers (from England and the continent), made innovations in stage lighting which affected all acting thereafter, and introduced scenic effects which were perfected and developed by Philip de Loutherbourg, whom he engaged to work for Drury Lane. He drove loungers from the stage, thus opening up possibilities for finer character delineation. On a quiet, uncluttered stage a hint, a look, a modest gesture could portray character at a stroke, more (often) than words and declamatory speeches could do. He strove for ensemble performance, the total effect of a play, and beyond that for the total effect of the whole evening's entertainment, from pre-performance music, to prologue, to mainpiece, to entr'acte song and dance, to amusing farce or pantomime as afterpiece, to epilogue—three hours of continuous and varied performance.

There was no aspect of the theatre, its audience, its supporting company of actors and house servants, its investments, taxes, supplies, wardrobe, food concessions, and public relations that he did not know fully, and did not in one way or another supervise. On the nights he appeared himself in a role, Drury Lane was full; sometimes crowds were turned away for lack of seats or standing room, and this state of affairs lasted for about thirty-five years. He also knew when to bow out, while all his powers and faculties were still high. He was vital, daring, and impudent; he was dedicated, persistent, and forthright; he was also (when occasion demanded) patient, compassionate, generous, cool, objective, cautious, and diplomatic, a man of understanding and judgment, of imagination and warmth. Had he not been the supreme professional and the vivacious force in the theatre of his time, there would be no point in writing his biography at full length. We are concerned less, I suppose, with peddling his personality than with presenting him as the master in his field, one who gave a major thrust to artistic theatrical performance of the best in English drama.

Professor Kahrl and I have long thought that now, with access to total evidence, a new sifting and reassessment is due. What evidence? It is massive, for it involves Garrick in all of his relationships, and especially with the theatre—for Garrick was the theatre, and the theatre was Garrick, for about a third of the eighteenth century. I recently counted my call slips alone for use in the Folger, the Huntington, the British Museum, the Royal College of Music, the Library of Congress, and the New York and Boston Public and Harvard Libraries, and they came to five hundred and eleven items of critical commentary by Garrick's contemporaries (varying in length from a paragraph of praise or blame to pamphlets of fifty to seventy-five pages each). Add to these the day-by-day account of his every day appearance on the London stage from 1741 through 1776 (four volumes), two volumes of his own verse (mainly Prologues and Epilogues), four volumes of his own plays, three well-edited volumes of his nearly 1,400 letters, and two volumes of letters written to him, coupled with hundreds of prints and paintings, both portraits and depictions of him in various roles, thirteen biographies, and a host of modern articles of specialized scholarship, and the task of

9

absorbing, understanding, selecting, and setting forth a lively picture of the man, in his eighteenth-century milieu, is challenging and exciting. But that's what scholarship is all about.

When I was in the early stages of graduate study, over forty years ago, a book which excited us all, even within the confines of Harvard Yard, the home of the Kittredges, Lowes's, and Robinsons, was John Matthews Manly's word from Chicago (of all places) called *Some New Light on Chaucer*.[4] Who would have thought that new things could be told 525 years after Chaucer's death, especially after the moguls of the Modern Language Association had been working with Chaucer with meticulous care since 1883! Yet some fragments came to light, and some re-arrangements of thinking about that remarkable poet came about as a result of some re-interpretations based upon the discoveries. It seemed fascinating at the time, not because it sprang from a fertile imagination in John Matthews Manly, but because it was based on the sound advance of recent scholarship. Our new light, we hope, will be reflected from a similar process. The evidence is massive, much of it not brought out before, and our light is a new perspective which this mass of evidence affords and demands.

Professor Kahrl and I are collaborating, he to do the personal and social life of the actor, and I to do the professional career of Garrick's acting, managing, and playwriting. Long good friends with shared interests, we have by necessity worked in both areas, but have concentrated in the allied but different fields. We feel somewhat qualified to go about this work together because in 1963 each of us completed thirty years of study and publication as a sort of preparation. He, after working that length of time, completed his three-volume, magnificently edited edition of Garrick's 1,362 letters, on which he had collaborated with the late David M. Little and others.[5] Through this process and intimate acquaintanceship with Garrick and all the people mentioned in his letters, and all their letters to him, Kahrl probably knows more about (and can command the resources for telling about) Garrick's personal life than any living scholar. I, after working a similar length of time, and after collaborating with four other American scholars, published my part (three volumes) of a day-by-day account of the *London Stage* (1747–1776), the period of Garrick's regime.[6] These volumes, like those of the letters, comprise a factual primary source book, taken entirely from the documents of the time. They deal with the pressures on actors and dramatists, the physical facilities of the theatres, their financing, management, and operation, their advertising, the makeup of the companies, benefit performances, costume, scenery, music, dance, repertory, specialty acts, production, audience, and the course of contemporary criticism. What was fragmentary for previous biographers is now, in the *Letters* and the *London Stage,* gathered into a huge and complete set of references. So we have an advantageous start.

What are some of the clear, if not absolutely new, lights which will form our directional signals? Well, Professor Kahrl, through leads in the letter documentation, is developing a fresh story of the young Garrick and his Lichfield attachment. What a pervading, long-continuing attachment that was, even to the sophisticated London actor and cosmopolitan. The pattern of life in the English countryside established there, the influence of the people and of rural England, lasted. Professor Kahrl is also re-examining Garrick's relationships with the circle of literary, business, and political friends; Garrick in France; Garrick the connoisseur of art; and Garrick's contributions to literary scholarship in the age by means of his great collection of 1,200 early English plays, which he ultimately bequeathed to the British Museum. Kahrl has spent the last ten years examining each of these plays in the British Museum, and Garrick's concern that they be used by Johnson, Steevens, Capel, and later Malone, and any scholar, as a matter of fact, who wished to look into them.[7]

Kahrl's detailed annotated catalogue with its 150-page introduction is being published by the British Museum this spring. Revolutionary indeed, it demonstrates a dimension of Garrick's interests and achievements unknown to and untouched by earlier biographers. Freshness will emerge here, as indeed it will when Kahrl writes of Garrick's relationship with half a dozen remarkable women of the century. His theme

11

will be that a highly developed culture is one in which men and women meet as equals, discussing the issues as well as the gossip which seemed important. Mrs. Cibber, Mrs. Clive, Mlle. Clairon, Madam Riccoboni, Lady Spencer, Fanny Burney, Elizabeth Montagu, Mrs. Griffith, Charlotte Lennox, and Hannah More will there be viewed.

I have done a chapter on the prevailing acting theory and practices of the time when Garrick first appeared, to show what he did (and how) to alter them; four chapters on the early, middle, and late stages of Garrick's theatre management, one on his own plays and adaptations, and one each on the impact of his great comic and great tragic roles. We'll conclude jointly on the man that emerges from these sequences: the professional, and the *honnête homme* of the age of enlightenment. In the new light of clearly accumulated fact, one can move with more assurance than before, when one sees the triumph in Garrick's acting of a strict professionalism, a know-how, and a concern for standards, bending its every effort towards illuminating the particular humour, difference, idiosyncratic identifying feature of each character, as opposed to demonstrating what we might call "aria perfection," or startling interpretations of such abstract universals as love, fear, hate, jealousy, rage, and the like. The books and rhetorical precedents had long demonstrated ways for expressing these universals. When universals were acted well the performance was applauded. But, more often than not, by Garrick's time performance became routine, mechanical, hackneyed, and dull.

We can illustrate by a parallel today (in the best of this sort of performance) in the field of opera. A Madam Caballé, singing in a tongue which half the audience cannot understand and concerned more with the quality of voice in an aria than with the consecutive action of the story, can stop the *Sicilian Vespers* for a full five minutes with her aria in the third act, to the tumultuous applause of the audience. Its enjoyment comes from listening to the trained voice come forth with power and modulation, rise to unthinkable heights, and descend with perfection to moving depths. Garrick could do a parallel performance on stage—it was called a "turn" of

12

the passions in which the excellent actor moved from fear, to hate, to rage; or from lust, to love, to tenderness. More often than not Garrick did this sort of thing in drawing-room performances of excerpts (when he was in Paris) of Macbeth's "turn" from imagination to resolution with the air-drawn daggers, or with Sir John Brute's shift from drunken brutality to sleep. But even in these, evidence becomes overwhelming that Garrick wrought a change in this style and manner, moving from the universal to the particular—a move called by his contemporaries "natural acting." This shift had a profound and long-lasting impact upon acting. It influenced Diderot mightily in developing his own theory of acting in his *Paradoxe sur le comédien.*

In his earlier years Diderot believed a great actor was one possessing an unusual amount of sympathetic understanding, able to lose self-consciousness completely in the passions of the character he was portraying. After seeing Garrick act, he developed a new theory. He seemed to see in Garrick one who studied his role well, yet while playing never lost control, so that he was able to make the audience believe he became the character he was portraying. The paradox, wrote Diderot, "is that in touching or amusing scenes the actor must be devoid of feeling; while he must appear to suffer, he must not suffer, while seeming to grow excited, he must remain cool. He must possess such judgment that he carries within himself an unmoved disinterested onlooker. He must have penetration and no sensibility, the art of mimicking everything, the art of rendering so exactly the outward signs of feeling that the audience falls into the trap."[8]

Garrick performed at least 2,500 times on stage.[9] What about Garrick the man amid all this acting? How would you, or I, or anyone know what we were as persons if we acted as many times, performing the special idiosyncrasies of ninety different characters? Only, one suspects, by developing a supreme professionalism, a professionalism which took work, work, work (plus a leavening genius), and *not* by the spontaneous overflow of powerful feeling, or a stumbling realistic naturalism, but by setting and maintaining standards of per-

13

fection, and by practicing ways by which to attain those standards. Definition, supported by examples, of this professionalism is a task I have taken on in presenting Garrick. Two aspects inevitably come up: a) the actor's preparation for his interpretations, and b) descriptions of the effect of the interpretations by those who sat nightly in pit, box, or gallery, and were moved by Garrick and his company. One of the best of these descriptions occurs in J. G. Noverre's *Letters on Dancing and Ballet* (No. IX). Garrick became his model, and changed for him the whole nature of ballet performance, from symbolic stylization to free-flowing acting where gesture, especially of the arms, and facial expression keyed to the "natural" became paramount. "Garrick is so natural," he wrote, "his expression has so much truth in it, his gesture, his facial expression, his very glance, are so eloquent, so persuasive that even those who understand not a word of English comprehend without difficulty the scene enacted before them."[10]

In his individual performance Garrick, of course, grew (remarkable though he was at the very outset) to a stature that commanded the respect of all. And this growth came about not entirely from within. He received and responded well to the criticism of those whose voices counted. Macklin saw him in Lear when he was but twenty-four years old, and wrote at length criticizing the performance. Macklin's voice was worth listening to. He thought that Garrick did not then sufficiently enter into the infirmities of a man of fourscore and upwards. In the repetition of the curse he began too low and ended too high. He lacked kingly dignity in the prison scene, and was defective in speaking the lines

> Now will we steal upon those sons-in-law
> And then kill—kill—kill!

by raising his voice in the first part too high, and letting it down too much in the last line. Garrick took the criticism to heart, and within six-weeks' time performed the role again to the complete amazement of Macklin. He said "it exceeded all his imagination; and [the curse] had such an effect, that

14

it seemed to electrify the audience with horror. The words, 'Kill, kill, kill,' echoed the revenge of the frantic King; whilst he exhibited such a scene of the pathetic on discovering his daughter Cordelia, as drew tears of commiseration from the whole house."[11]

But Garrick ultimately wanted more. It now appears clearly that he hoped for and worked for excellent ensemble performance, where each actor and actress remained in character until the final curtain, and contributed by every look, speech, and gesture to the total impact of the whole performance. He moved professionally towards this goal by precept, by compulsion, and by example. For the first he held regular readings of plays in the Green room before casting the parts, showing all there gathered how each part might be acted to fit in with the thrust of the play.[12] For the second he set up rigid forfeits of salary for those who missed rehearsals. Mrs. Clive complained that she was required to come in from Twickenham at a cost of £5 to rehearse a part, the lines of which she could say in her sleep.[13] Garrick persuaded her (as he had Mrs. Cibber earlier) that she was needed for the sake of the rest of the actors so that all in the play could together get the sense of the whole.[14] For the third he took on minor parts himself, such as Abel Drugger the tobacconist in Jonson's *Alchemist,* Lady Bountiful's servant Scrub in *The Beaux' Stratagem,* and Fribble in his own *Miss in Her Teens,* to demonstrate the professional importance of every character in every play. When processions formed integral parts of an afterpiece, he walked in them himself whenever he required other top actors to do so. For the final performance of his acting career he played not Lear or Hamlet but Don Felix in Mrs. Centlivre's *The Wonder; or a Woman Keeps a Secret.* The leading role therein is *not* Don Felix but Violante, a woman who not only keeps a secret, but manipulates the boyish, super-proud, essentially immature Felix in most entertaining fashion.

I have mentioned his driving loungers from the stage, a matter of importance to theatre history, but also (in his approach to that directive) revealing, biographically. "Gentlemen" were privileged at the time, in recompense for extra sums they paid for entrance, to sit on stage and wander behind the scenes. They were an artistic nuisance, but an economic advantage, especially on benefit nights. Garrick had a hideous experience with one of them in his early years of acting in Ireland. As Thomas Sheridan tells it, "Garrick performed the character of King Lear. Mrs. Woffington that of Cordelia. Just as they prepared themselves for the drawing of the scene, which was to discover the old king asleep with his head in the lap of Cordelia, a Gentleman threw himself down on the other side of the fair princess, and without the least regard for her rank began to treat her with utmost indecency. Resentment followed on her part, and abuse on his. Mr. Garrick was silent (he was twenty-five years old at the time) but could not help casting an eye of indignation at so brutal a scene, which was considered so daring an insult by the Gentleman, that he and two more of his comrades searched the house for him after the play, vowing with dreadful imprecations that they would put him to death."[15] This was in 1742. Twenty years later Garrick, remembering this, but now in his full power, banished all loungers from the stage, thus insuring not only diminution of insult but a quiet stage where (with new lighting and new scenery) further concentration on character delineation could come about. This banishment and resulting improvement of characterization on stage begat a new and far-reaching thrust in dramatic criticism in the pamphlets of the age.

Heretofore such criticism had been judicial in nature, weighing and balancing the "Beauties" and the "Faults" of performance, and evaluating its aesthetic appeal by a sort of mechanical summation of the preponderance of the one or the other. Such a critical approach gave way, in Garrick's time and largely because of Garrick's performance, to interpretive criticism centering upon characterization, motivation, role relationships within the plot, and all that we expect today in enlightened dramatic comment.[16]

Some clear shafts of new light now also appear in many other areas of Garrick's activity as manager: his insistence upon a definition of duties, responsibilities, and authority between himself and his partner James Lacy; his establishing a structure of viable communication within the Drury Lane company membership, as well as with the audience, the wide audience of the whole "Town" (public relations if you will); his delegation of duties; his policies and practices in recruiting (continued from 1747 to 1776) of new actors, dancers, and musicians. We now know that he interviewed and accepted (during his quarter century of management) 584 persons who wished to perform, and that he was particularly interested in bringing on and bringing up troupes of child actors, and in giving youth a start. His interviews with persons rejected are unrecorded (save a few cases), but may have been countless. He yielded to no pressures from outsiders in recruitment. A letter to the Duchess of Portland, now hanging englassed in the reception room of the Garrick Club in London, bears eloquent testimony to this fact:

Madam: I shall always be happy to obey Your Grace's commands, but our company at present is so full, and all the parts dispos'd of, that I could not without great injustice to those actors I have already engag'd, employ the person you recommended.

I have given Mr. Collins the best advice in my power, & assur'd him that I shall be ready at the end of the season to examine his qualifications for the stage. If Your Grace will permit me to speak my mind, I think he has the most unpromising Aspect for an actor I ever saw—a small pair of unmeaning eyes stuck in a round unthinking face are not the most desirable requisites for a hero, or a fine gentleman—however I will give him a tryal if he is unemploy'd at that time of the year, & if he can be of the least service to me or himself, I shall most certainly obey Your Grace's commands. . . .[17]

After he had been managing for fifteen years, his proteges and the actors trained by him were themselves managing theatres in Dublin, Edinburgh, York, Cheltenham, Liverpool, Bath, Bristol, and Richmond, and were having a powerful impact at Covent Garden and the Haymarket in London, too.[18] We can now name names and spot positions, and follow the continuing relationships of this network of performing and managing artists. This development is all part of the vital

17

leadership which Garrick gave to the performing arts in that century.

Garrick's two-year sojourn in France and Italy advanced no end his long-simmering interest in changing the physical aspects of Drury Lane Theatre to provide conditions in which novelty, artistry, and variety might flourish. Basic to everything else was improved stage lighting. He improved it, balancing light from the wings with that from footlights. One reviewer noted that Garrick had created artificial day, another that he had brought the milky way to the foot of the stage.[19] All that the nineteenth-century introduction of gaslight and electricity could do was to modify Garrick's illumination in degree. Lighting changes meant new possibilities for scenic design—transparencies, cutaways, differing levels, depths, perspectives, and angles, hence enter the Alsatian artist de Loutherbourg.[20] In the wake of these improvements came insistence upon improved costuming—elegance, style, difference, and beauty, even the faint beginnings of historical accuracy and appropriateness. Cibber had rented most of his stage props. Garrick built or purchased his, rearranging them for use in different plays.[21]

Having to deal, as manager, with the personnel problems that his brother George (deputized to handle this department) could not solve, and as a person warm and sympathetic to people and their frustrations, he was quick to establish and make work (when he returned from his French tour) a Fund for Decayed Actors, a sort of pension and health insurance, contributed to by each full-time actor earning a certain salary on an agreed-upon ratio. The Fund was measurably increased by the proceeds of an annual "clear" benefit performance. On these occasions Garrick played himself, cast his best actors in excellent plays *(Hamlet, Richard III, Lear, The Stratagem, The Wonder)* with income passing the £300 mark, an average full house bringing £160 to £180. Garrick himself wrote (and had printed at his own expense sufficient copies for each member of Parliament) a proposed Bill (which was introduced, read, and voted) to legalize and make financially viable and accountable this Theatrical Fund. Thus the aged, the sick,

18

and the actors' widows would have help from the profession.

Garrick as a professional dramatist was not one whose texts show lustre when anthologized to be studied in the classroom. He was a playwright of remarkable ability who wrote, or adapted, or had a major hand in sixty-eight pieces, each of which was popular on the stage of his time. Our new biographical perspective on these plays emphasizes his interest and experimentation with musical drama, and his care in adapting the older English plays, especially those of Shakespeare and Jonson. Word somehow got about in the twentieth century that Garrick was tone deaf and cared not for "sing-song" plays. The facts point to different conclusions. We cannot vouch for the physiological structure of his ear, but he wrote lyrics for over 109 songs, engaged the best composers to set them, did nine musical plays, and sent audience after audience out into the night air humming a tune, holding in memory a rhyme, and elongating a sense of amusement.

He actually became a playwright before he became an actor, and singing was prominent in his first piece, *Lethe* (1740). This satirical skit presents a half a dozen types—a drunk, a termagant, a "Fine Lady," a poet, a tailor, a female writer, etc.—who come to the famous river of the underworld to drink the waters, forget their troubles, and start anew. Garrick wrote lyrics for two songs therein, one for the leading tenor of the day, John Beard, and one for the charming but boisterous Mrs. Clive. Both songs became popular in the sheet-music trade, the words sung and the tunes hummed in the London streets beyond the walls of Drury Lane. He continued writing lyrics until the end. Some sang themselves, especially those in anapestic verse, but all were "set" to music by the competent composers of the time, the Arnes, the Dibdins, the Boyces, the Oswalds, Aylwards, Battishills, and Barthelemons of the day.

Garrick brought on stage a young Jewish boy, Master Michael Leoni, with an astounding voice, and wrote for him a musical play, *The Enchanter* (1760), with music composed by J. C. Smith, Handel's pupil. Near the close of his career he commissioned Dr. T. A. Arne to set to music his *May Day, or the Little Gipsey* (1775), in which he brought forward a young Jewish girl, Harriet Abrams, whose tremulous soprano had great appeal. In the intervening years he experimented with seven other musical plays. His managerial budget for music at Drury Lane for his twenty-one-piece orchestra increased steadily. A whole new world of joint cooperative scholarship in the performing arts opens up here for musicologists and theatre historians, now that we have at hand the entire and detailed record of performances, and now that the music itself is being reassembled.[22] A new Garrick steps forth in this field, or a new dimension of the well-known Garrick.

He was a continuing, genuine, and resourceful experimenter. Though professing to "put down" Pantomime as a form of show not appealing to the reason, but gratifying to surprise and a desire for rapid scenic changes, Garrick tried his hand at this form, producing (with the novelty of a speaking Harlequin) one of the most popular of pantomimes, *Harlequin's Invasion* (1759). Its amusing and whimsically imaginative story reaches its high point when the forces of pantomime are set to invade Parnassus, the realm of Shakespeare, and are defeated. But the Garrick dialogue soars. Clown Simon asks Harlequin (who has risen unexpectedly from the ground before him in all his particolors), "Pray, friend Whirligig, what profession are you of?"

> *Harlequin:* A fly catcher—I was formerly altogether among the stars—I plied as ticket-porter in the milky Way, and carried the Howdyes from one planet to another; but finding that too fatiguing I got into the service of the Rainbow, and now I wear his livery. Don't you think I fib now, Friend Simon? (I, iii).

The Pantomime was performed again, and again, and again. So successful was it that Garrick, with the aid of his prompter William Hopkins, put together another pantomime called *Harlequin's Jacket.* The conventional attitude has been to apologize for the appearance of these entertainments in the Garrick canon. What we now can do is examine them in the light of his total commitment to the stage.

20

The publication of *all* the Garrick letters, including those carrying his rejections of about eighty plays, allows us to extract his theory of the *vis comica* (comic force) and of tragic effectiveness. The standards he marked out were conventional, but pragmatically sound. Plot was the most important factor, but in tragedy motivation had to be accomplished by the striking, the pathetic, and the terrible. The whole context had to be so written as to enable the skilled actor to interpret character convincingly. Garrick once told Baron Grimm that Racine, "so beautiful and enchanting to read, cannot be acted, because he says everything, and leaves the actor nothing to do."[23] In 1754 he rejected John Cleland's "Vespasian" for lacking motivation,[24] and in 1772 wrote Boswell that his friend Mickle's *Siege of Marseilles* would not do. Why? "Speeches and mere poetry will no more make a play than planks and timbers in the dockyard can be called a ship. . . . It is fable, passion, and action which constitute a tragedy, and without them we might as well exhibit one of Tillotson's sermons."[25]

In comedy it was action, action, action that counted. A now-to-be-seen relationship appears between Garrick's dramatic theory and his performance practice, namely, his insistence in practice upon ensemble acting (with all actors remaining in character until the final curtain), and his insistence in theory that total plot structure must be evident. But within the plot structure each actor must interpret excellently. As the German visitor G. C. Lichtenberg remarked of Garrick's artistic distinctions in performing, "On stage Garrick makes use of lore which one would almost pronounce wasted on such surroundings. . . . if he were representing, for example, a great glutton, and wanted to feel with his fingers to see whether his capon or pheasant on the spit was done to a turn, I dare swear he would probe with the fourth finger of his left hand. In all others there would be too much strength, and too little feeling."[26]

We feel that the need for a new biography is ample. The problems inevitable in collaborating are several, but Kahrl and I are agreed that a full portrait of the man, rather than a fragmented series of studies on his special attributes related to specialized subjects, is the soundest approach. The challenge is fascinating—reviving a man for whom so many now possess so many stereotyped ideas, which indeed we question; avoiding the tendency to sentimentalize and romanticize, as we assemble a thousand or two stark facts (none of which turn out to be stark or simple); and selecting for pertinent emphasis. For to see the man in his age is to bring to bear on him the currents of ideas in his time, religious, scientific, economic, political, philosophical, and artistic. Such an approach could mean the inclusion of extended vignettes of many other people whose lives impinged on Garrick, as his did on theirs. Control of the lively subject matter and selection are obviously called for.

What sort of man is revealed to Professor Kahrl, for example, in the rich material of the 1,362 letters alone, and to what sort of a milieu do they respond? As one reads halfway through the first volume of letters, one feels he is viewing through Garrick's eyes the endless oddity of human behavior as it showed itself in the eighteenth century. By the end of that volume and on into the second, the revelation turns inward, and one's focus directs itself to the seemingly predictable character of Garrick's behavior. Yet, is he a cool extrovert, or intense and thin-skinned beneath what must have seemed to his contemporaries to have been a charming carelessness?

His earliest letters, when a boy of seventeen, suggest that mixture of serious responsibility and whimsicality evident throughout his life—respectful to his father, conciliatory to his elder brother, determined as to his own career, flattered but not swell-headed by the unbelievable success of his first stage appearances. The liveliness, wit, and teasing humor of his early family letters yield to a new seriousness and wrangling as he bids for the management of Drury Lane, followed by a continued edginess concerning his lifelong partners James and Willoughby Lacy. Yet he pauses often, over the years, to examine himself, or at least to state again and again what sort of a fellow he thought he was. To Francis Hayman, the artist: "I have no luke-warmness in my Temper, & as I am naturally open and Impetuous, it is a necessary prudence in me to shun Company I am doubtfull of."[27] As he grew in the acting profession he was sure he was perfecting something new. He predicted to the Countess of Burlington in 1750 that Colley Cibber's granddaughter Jane would not succeed as Jane Shore because old Colley was training her up in an outmoded style. "She . . . may have Genius for ought I know," wrote he, "but if she has, it is so eclipsed by the Manner of Speaking the Laureat has taught her, that I am afraid it will not do. We differ greatly in our Notions of Acting . . . & If he is right, I am, & ever shall be in the wrong road."[28]

After his marriage, especially during the summers of 1749 through the mid-1750s when the closed theatre failed to absorb his excessive energies, his correspondence with Lady Burlington's family increases, and gets somewhat sticky—family gossip, master-servant relationships in a noble household, seemed to fascinate him. But ere he got too involved he stood off and looked at himself, with that same whimsy that stood him in good stead from the beginning. He wrote at the time to Benjamin Wilson,[29] "I am continually fighting of Shadows, & am left like poor Shirly in the *Rehearsal*—

> Hey ho! hey day!
> I know not what to do, or what to say—"

Through the 1750 decade his competition at Covent Garden was great, and his theatre management battles were formidable. His nervous energies became exhausted, and his mercurial temper flared at the close of the 1762–63 season, when he decided to chuck the theatre and take an extended trip to France and Italy. New scenes and new faces, adulation in Paris and Florence and Rome were restorative, until ill health in Italy sapped Mrs. Garrick's strength, and illness in Munich sapped his. But he always revived under praise: "You can't imagine, my dear Colman, what honours I have receiv'd from all kind of People here—the Nobles & the Litterati have made so much of Me that I am quite asham'd of opening my heart Ev'n to You."[30]

His appetite for news at all times of his life—political (he was a friend of Burke, Wilkes, and Generals Howe and Burgoyne), theatrical (from actors, actresses, managers, and spectators), literary, and journalistic (from England when in France, and from France when home in England)—was insatiable, and bespoke his relish of life in general. He kept abreast of all that was going on. In an age when news spread slowly, he gathered it and passed it along to his friends on the gallop. The word-of-mouth and private letter grapevine as sources for enjoying municipal and national affairs is underscored by the haste in which Garrick seemed always to be writing—"I write on the gallop," "I am on the go—," "The man is waiting—," "The coach leaves immediately—," "I write in a hurry surrounded by company." Like Chaucer's Merchant, "A busier man than he ther nowhere nas," Garrick's several statements of obvious exaggeration—"I am just rising from my bed of death"—seem to some today to be affected, but one soon sees that they reflected a mannerism closely tied to his theatrical life and high-strung nature.

Infighting and exasperation characterized some of the management correspondence, but he never held grudges for long. His circumspect relation with James Lacy often broke into a cry of "what goes on!" "Just give me a clue to walk into the labyrinth of Lacy's brain, that I may be upon my guard," he wrote to brother George.[31] But his fruitful friendships and pleasurable correspondence with Colman, Foote, Steevens, Burke, Gibbon, John Hoadly, the lawyer Patterson, the financiers James Clutterbuck, and Albany Wallis are beautifully and calmly expressed. Wanting his opponents to be satisfied, he often suggested that their discussions be conducted with third parties of their own choosing present. He was scrupulously fair and objective in such dealings. Busy, busy, busy, yet his retirement at the height of his powers brought a relief evident in the tone of his correspondence after 1776. He wrote to James Boswell (Kahrl, 1107), "No school Boy at a breaking up for the Holidays, had Ever Such rantipole Spirits—I feel such a Weight off my Spirits, that I really feel myself a New Man—however there is no good without some concomitant

Evil—I grow fat, & Short-winded." Few letters are more pleasant to read than those to the Countess Spencer during the last thirty months of his life, wherein he sports again and again with whimsy and good humor upon the creeping illness which destroyed him in early 1779.

The problems of the creative process lead both of us inevitably to the problem of *control* of the wide and rich material at our disposal. Where should the limit be? What kind of critical biography should we present, one which includes commentary on *all* Garrick ever wrote or ever said, or one which *refers* clearly to all such, but selects items of novel and significant importance in showing the man, the actor, manager, and dramatist whose impact in these many fields affected the course of stage history in England down to our own times? We have chosen the latter course, deeming it unnecessary to rework several dozen careful studies of Garrick's adaptations of earlier plays (for example), his detailed treatment of Shakespeare, his improvement or vast cutting of French farces, or to rehearse for the fourth time his aims, accomplishments, and shortcomings—in detail, that is—for the Stratford Jubilee.

Nevertheless, another major problem shows above the surface in the handling of an actor who was always growing, changing his style, reinterpreting his roles to keep them fresh and to show new layers of meaning in them. Such cannot be done well in summary. For instance, think what he did with the role of Macbeth over an acting span for the play of nearly a quarter of a century.

He early retrieved the Shakespearian text from the Davenant adaptation, which had held the stage since the late seventeenth century. The interpretation which he and Mrs. Pritchard gave to the leading roles astounded and intrigued all beholders. Many wrote to him about his specifically moving scenes. Thomas Davies recalled the general reaction to the murder-of-Duncan scene, one which Zoffany depicted with only moderate success:

His distraction of mind and agonizing horrors were finely contrasted by her seeming *apathy*. The beginning of the scene after the murder was conducted in terrifying whispers. Their looks and action supplied

25

the place of words. You heard what they spoke, but you learned more from the agitation of mind displayed in their action and deportment. The poet here gives only an outline to the consummate actor—'I have done the deed!—Dids't thou not hear a noise! When? Did you not speak?' The dark colouring given by the actor to these abrupt speeches makes the scene awful and tremendous. The wonderful expression of heartfelt horror, which Garrick felt when he showed his bloody hands can only be conceived and described by those who saw him.[32]

Apathy on her part, horror turning inward on his! One element of the tragedy of that play is the way in which these two, who have been close and loving at the outset, pull away from each other as the plot develops. She, a tigress at first, breaks and dies tormented. He, a thoughtful, engaging fellow at the outset, hardens as the play develops. When she dies, he reflects on the inevitability of that death, and the general mess of things, reflecting the numbness that has crept over their former relationship, and which breeds his contempt for existence. Garrick tells us in a letter that he gave the "out, out brief candle, life's but a walking shadow" speech with a most contemptuous indifference for life.[33] Yet the Reverend Samuel Knott recalled an instance in which Garrick pronounced that speech in "the softest voice that ever drew pity from the heart of man." "I well remember," he wrote, "[it] affected me beyond expression."[34] If so, we witness a change in performance, and a different look to the tragedy. Question for the biographer: what does such evidence reveal as to the nature of the man? How to express these shifting nuances, this continuing non-routine creativity? As a professional he knew that stereotypes grow dull with constant repetition.

Sifting, culling from remarks of contemporaries, selecting and highlighting may, perhaps, be the way to go about it. But the temptation is great to load it all in. We know from close search of the parish registers who Garrick's neighbors were for years in Southampton Street. They represented 113 different trades, with large concentrations among tailors, victuallers, peruke makers, shoemakers and apothecaries, jewellers, staymakers, bankers, and distillers. With these people

Garrick rubbed elbows daily and, mimic that he was, he observed each, catching now an attitude, now a gesture, now a shrug, now a wry smile, and again a limp or a determined stance. These hints he built upon and reproduced in seemingly effortless acting on stage. Lichtenberg wrote, "It is refreshing to see his manner of walking, shrugging his shoulders, putting his hands into his pockets, putting on his hat, now pulling it down over his eyes, and then pushing it sideways off his forehead, all this with so slight a movement of his limbs as though each were his right hand . . . Man was his study from the cultured and artificial denizens of the salons of St. James's down to the savage creatures in the eating houses of St. Giles."[35]

So—problems and processes—the *why* of a fourteenth biography, the *division of labor* between two collaborators, the approach to the *creative process,* the *control* of abundant material, *communication* of an *ever-changing* and freshening interpretation of roles—a *final* problem, which indeed may dissolve in the writing itself, concerns consonance of style. Do two collaborators write the same idiom, move with the same pace, submerge themselves successfully as they bring their biographee forward to center stage? That we shall have to see, but it may not be important, for Garrick is at all times to be front and center, and Garrick himself was indeed a chameleon, never quite the same at any moment. He could act an inebriated French peasant and fool the townspeople in Provence, could leave his box in Drury Lane and a moment later appear on stage in the character of an unreconstructed protester (unrecognizable at first even to his wife still in the box), could mimic a cat in the bushes for the merriment of George Colman's young son,[36] and yet could move packed houses to tears, and to an aesthetic experience deeper than tears, in a Hamlet, a Lear, a Richard, or a Macbeth. Our several styles may indeed contribute wholesomely to the kaleidoscopic effect.

But consonance of style between joint authors is probably minor in comparison with the major problem, and indeed the greatest potential value, of the biography of this best-known figure of the mid-eighteenth century. The challenge faces *every* biographer, and the probability of its being met successfully was long ago doubted by Walter Savage Landor in one of his more agreeable sonnets:

Tho panting in the play-hour of my youth
I drank of Avon, too, a dangerous draft
That roused within the feverish thirst for song,
Yet never may I trespas o'er the stream
Of jealous Acheron, nor alive descend
The silent and unsearchable abodes
Of Erebus and Night, nor unchastized
Lead up long absent heroes into day.
When on the pausing theatre of earth
Eve's shadowy curtain falls, can any man
Bring back the far-off intercepted hills,
Grasp the round rock-build turret, or arrest
The glittering spires that pierce the brow of heaven?
Rather can any with outstripping voice
The parting sun's gigantic strides recall?

Can we bring it off?

Well, we're on our way to try our luck at leading up a long-absent hero into day, as we try "the parting sun's gigantic strides" to recall. More feeling of regret passed through the intellectual circles of London in the early summer of 1776 at Garrick's departure from the stage than at the departure from the kingdom of those distant American colonies which were, about the same time, declaring their independence. This biography should at least be timely.

Notes

1. In order, the full biographies are Thomas Davies, *Memoirs of the Life of David Garrick* (London, 1780); Arthur Murphy, *The Life of David Garrick* (London, 1801); James Boaden, Preface to *The Private Correspondence of David Garrick with the most Celebrated Persons of his Time* (London, 1831–32); Percy Fitzgerald, *The Life of David Garrick* (London, 1868, and his revised edn, 1899); Joseph Knight, *David Garrick* (London, 1894) and his article on Garrick in the *DNB;* Mrs. Clement Parsons, *Garrick and his Circle* (London, 1906); Frank A. Hedgcock, *A Cosmopolitan Actor, David Garrick` and his French Friends* (London, 1912); Margaret Barton, *Garrick* (New York, 1949); Anna Byrd Stewart, *Enter David Garrick* (New York, 1952); Carola Oman, *David Garrick* (Hodder & Stoughton, 1958). A brief *Life* by one Leonatus (probably Davies) appeared in 1779 just after the actor's death.

2. Forster Collection (3322 F 3.C.12) "Clippings Relating to Garrick," Victoria and Albert Museum, No. 25. Ronald Paulson, in his *Hogarth: His Life, Art, and Times,* II, 342 (New Haven: Yale University Press, 1971), mentions variants of the story.

3. The "Cases" of Charles Macklin and Garrick were printed in full by Davies in his *Memoirs, cit.* They were issued to the town in separate pamphlets and rejoinders in 1743.

4. New York: Holt, 1926.

5. *The Letters of David Garrick,* ed. by David M. Little and George M. Kahrl (London, Oxford University Press, 1963), three vols., referred to hereafter as Kahrl plus a number, which refers to the number of the letter as serialized in the volumes.

6. *The London Stage, 1660–1800:* A Calendar of Plays, Entertainments & Afterpieces, together with Casts, Box Receipts, and Contemporary Comment, compiled from the Playbills, Newspapers, and Theatrical Diaries of the period, in five parts (Carbondale: Southern Illinois University Press, 1961–68). Pertinent findings in Part 3, Vol II, ed A. H. Scouten (1741–1747) and Part 4, Vols I, II, III, ed G. W. Stone, Jr. (1747–1776).

7. J. G. Noverre, father of modern ballet, had the run of these books and also the rest of Garrick's fine library. See *The Chevalier Noverre*, by Deryck Lynham (London: Sylvan Press, 1950) pp. 41, 141.

8. Denis Diderot, *Paradoxe sur le comédien*, 1770.

9. Note 6 above, *passim*.

10. *Chevalier Noverre, op. cit.*, p. 141, and Noverre's *Lettres sur la danse* No. IX (1760).

11. William Cooke, *Memoirs of Charles Macklin* (London, 1804), 107.

12. See Davies *Memoirs, cit.*, 1,149 (1808 edn.); and *Dramatic Miscellanies* (Dublin, 1784) II, 41 ff., re the casting of *Every Man in his Humour*.

13. Boaden, *Private Correspondence, cit.* I, 203–204.

14. Kahrl, Ltr 247 to Mrs. Cibber 24 Jan 1760: "The Comedy *(The Way to Keep Him)* will require four or five regular Rehearsals at least, and tho *You* may be able to appear with two, Yet I am afraid the rest . . . will be perplex'd and disjointed if they have not the advantage of your Character to Rehearse with them." See also Kahrl, ltr 445, where Garrick out of town at Hampton was faced with a command performance of Oakly in *The Jealous Wife*, which he had not played for years, wrote brother George *not* for the script of Oakly's lines alone, but for the *whole* prompt book, to prepare him for rehearsing three days later in London.

15. See Thomas Sheridan, *An Humble Appeal to the Public* (Dublin, 1758), p. 52.

16. "David Garrick's Significance in the History of Shakespearean Criticism," *PMLA,* LXV (March, 1750), 183–197, by G. W. Stone, Jr.

17. The Garrick Club letter: see Kahrl 476 (29 October 1767). Perhaps Garrick did Collins a favor, for he became a most successful monologist. See *A Biographical Dictionary of Actors*, Highfill, Burnim, and Langhans (Carbondale: Southern Illinois University Press, 1973).

18. Actors such as Henry Woodward (at CG and Dublin); John Beard (at CG); Henry Mossop (Dublin); John Palmer (Bath); Richard Yates (Liverpool); David Ross and James Love (Edinborough); Love (at Richmond); Thomas King (at Bristol); Winstone and Clarke (at Jacob Wells Theatre in Bristol); William Powell (at CG); Parsons (at Bristol); Spranger Barry (at Liverpool for a time). See *London Stage*, Part 4, I, Introduction p. xcix.

19. *Public Advertiser,* 25 Sept 1765. See also *David Garrick, Director,* by Kalman Burnim (Pittsburgh: University of Pittsburgh Press, 1961), 78–83.

20. See "The Stage Spectacles of Philip de Loutherbourg," Dissertation by Ralph G. Allen (Yale, 1960), University Microfilm Xerox.

21. See bills for properties in Folger Shakespeare Library, and Raymond J. Pentzell, "Garrick's Costuming," *Theatre Survey,* X (May, 1969), 18–40.

22. Much may be found in the British Museum, the Royal College of Music, the Library of Congress, the Folger Library, and some separate songs published monthly in the *London Magazine* and *Westminster Magazine* (1748–1776).

23. *Correspondence Littéraire,* 1765, quoted in F. A. Hedgcock, *op. cit.,* p. 234.

24. Kahrl, 689.

25. Kahrl, 677.

26. *Lichtenberg's Visits to England as Described in his Letters and Diaries,* trans. and annotated by M. L. Mare and W. H. Quarrell (Oxford: Clarendon Press, 1938), p. 9.

27. Kahrl, 47.

28. *Ibid.,* 97.

29. *Ibid.,* 231.

30. *Ibid.,* 317.

31. *Ibid.,* 459.

32. *Dramatic Miscellanies* (Dublin, 1784), II, 93.

33. Kahrl, 281.

34. Boaden I, 377–378.

35. *Lichtenberg's Visits to England, op. cit.,* pp 7–8.

36. *Random Records,* by George Colman the Younger (London, 1830), I, 119.

II

A Peep behind the Curtain: Mass Theatrical Biography

PHILIP H. HIGHFILL, JR.

THAT WIT'S WIT, the late John Crow, used to throw library attendants who had not experienced his drolleries into nervous panic by going to the reading room desk and fiercely demanding the scissors and paste. It was John's satirical way of making fun of the disdain which some critical scholars affect toward any study which involves the collection of many facts from many sources. The "scissors-and-paste" reproach surely hovered over our *Dictionary*[1] all those long years before publication. Our materials are certainly "fracted and corroborate," in both Pistol's and the correct signification of both words. Hospitably housed in the Folger Shakespeare Library for 21 years, the materials have grown until there are now perhaps 190,000 5x8 cards, in main and ancillary files; and although we have employed no paste, we have unblushingly plied the computer and the photocopier.

To what end have my two colleagues and I squirreled away these shards and pebbles from the past? Why will we have invested in this enterprise, along with other duties, more than sixty scholar-years by the time we proof the final volume? Is there justification beyond normal scholars' curiosity for spending hundreds of thousands of dollars on an attempt to revivify gestures so long faded from mortal memory, voices so many years stilled, of people most of whom have for long been utterly unknown? What are the sources of such mass biography? What are its characteristic problems? I would like to try to answer these questions, as much for my own interest as yours, for this is my first pause for retrospection over the long road that we have traveled.

35

Biography, ridden by hagiology and inaccuracy, had not often been an honored genre before just about the time of the Restoration—nearly simultaneously—of Charles II and the drama to England. And in its full-dress form, except for the works of Roger North and a handful of others, it did not amount to much as art before Samuel Johnson. But I deplore especially the fact that *compendious* and *collected* biography, of the sort which bloomed briefly from about 1650 to 1690 in the bright pages of John Aubrey, Thomas Fuller, Anthony à Wood, and Gerard Langbaine, did not take a theatrical direction, and, indeed, that virtually no one before Boswell made use of some of the methods of that interesting quartet. How helpful it would have been to our researches if collected brief biography in the manner and with a combination of the techniques of those good gossips had developed and had taken actors for its subject matter.

Thomas Fuller, in his preface to *The History of the Worthies of England* (1662), spoke of his effort "to entertain the reader with delight: I confess, the subject is but dull in itself, to tell the time and place of men's birth, and deaths, their names, with the number of their books; and therefore this bare skeleton of time, place and person must be fleshed with some pleasant passages. To this intent I have purposely interlaced (not as meat, but as condiment) many delightful stories, that so the reader, if he do not arise, which I hope and desire, *religiosor* or *doctior,* with more piety or learning, at least he may depart *jocundior,* with more pleasure and lawful delight." Anthony à Wood's *Athenae Oxonienses, An Exact History of all the Writers who have had their Education in . . . Oxford from . . . 1500 . . .* reflects the almost Boswellian ingenuity with which he approached his task. James Harrington declared, in his Preface to the first edition of the *Athenae Oxonienses,* that Wood had

not only consulted all the Registers relating to the University but all other Writings and Records, Ms. and printed, whether in the Tower, Exchequer, Paper Office, or elsewhere, that could give him any notices of these Authors, or let him into the true knowledge of their Lives, Performances, and Writings. The Registers of the

36

ancient Churches and Cathedrals were diligently consulted; the Wills of the deceas'd persons were at the Prerogative Office examin'd; the Windows of Churches, Epitaphs and Inscriptions, have been search'd; the Genealogy of Authors at the Heralds Office hath been inquir'd into; and no method hath been unattempted which could contribute to a true History of these Writers, or ascertain the least date and circumstance of their lives.

Fuller's taste, Wood's scholarly conscience—what a pity they were not applied to theatrical contemporaries.

It very nearly happened. The next year after the publication of the *Athenae,* Gerard Langbaine published *An Account of the English Dramatick Poets.* Just as, after many ages, hagiography gave way to ecclesiastical biography, and that was succeeded by lives of secular Worthies, and those accounts were followed by lives of people not necessarily worthy, but all of them authors, Langbaine isolated *dramatic* authors. Except for the scurrilous verses that taunted them in life and the overblown marmoreal sentiments which were sometimes granted them after death by noble lovers or patrons, few mere performers earned even the dubious favor of a sensationalized short biographical notice in the seventeenth century.

It would please me to be able to report that in the eighteenth century biography kept pace with the developments in acting, directing, and stagecraft, or even that it lagged not far behind other biography. But I cannot. *Both Theatres Opened a History of the lives of the most noted actors and actresses . . . by a gentleman conversant with them in five reigns* (c. 1727) was very short and prudently anonymous. Nearly forty years later, in 1764, David Erskine Baker in his *Companion to the Play-house* combined the interests of Langbaine and the anonymous gentleman by granting space to "the lives of our most celebrated actors, who were likewise authors of any theatrical composition." But the eighteenth century was three-quarters over before any sustained interest was shown in collecting the lives of actors *as a professional class.*

In 1772 the anonymous *Theatrical Biography; or, Memoirs of the Principle Performers of the Three Theatres Royal . . .* contained 44 brief biographies of performers and achieved two editions.

In 1786 a pamphlet of 64 pages, *The Green-Room Mirror. Clearly delineating our present theatrical performers* . . . was published anonymously, as were its successors *The Secret History of the Green Rooms* of 1790, 1792, 1793, and 1795, and *Crosby's Pocket Companion to the Playhouses,* 1796. Also in 1796 appeared *Roach's Authentic Memoirs of the Green Room,* which had five editions before 1814. Wally C. Oulton usurped Roach's title in a collection of 1799. There were two editions—1802, 1805—of *The Thespian Dictionary,* and Thomas Gilliland published *The Dramatic Mirror* in 1808. Isaac Reed had in 1782 expanded Baker's original compilation, and in 1812 Stephen Jones published a further expansion. William Oxberry's *Dramatic Biography and Histrionic Anecdotes,* published by his widow in 1827, completes the brief roster of publications which could by the utmost courtesy be called biographical dictionaries of performers in our period.

Those things are not as bad as they have been represented. Some even contain skeptical warnings about the aristocratic pasts and fancy connections invented by the press-agentry of the time. And for a few of our people they are all that we have to depend on except performance records. Brief, invariably vague on dates, allusive, often biased, their most serious deficiency is the way they overlap, both in respect of cribbing each others' facts and phraseology, and in respect of celebrating much the *same* corps of actors of the mid-to-late century— perhaps no more than two hundred persons in all. In any case, they were impervious to the developing standards of historicity, and they did not do the respectable service for show people that, for instance, Benjamin Hutchinson did for medical men in *Biographia Medica* of 1780 or that John Charnock did for naval officers in *Biographia Navalis* of 1794–1798.

Between the first quarter of the eighteenth century and the second quarter of the nineteenth, there were also produced some seventy-five or eighty longer biographies (including Colley Cibber's marvelous *Apology*), varying wildly in size and degree of credibility, of about fifty actors and singers on the British stage, from Francis Abington, Philip Astley, Anthony Aston, Sophia Baddeley, and John Bannister, to Thomas

Weston, Tate Wilkinson, Robert Wilks, Margaret Woffington, and Mary Wrighten. From those volumes, if we employ the due care which I shall presently emphasize, we can quarry much solid building material, not only about their primary subjects but also about associated people. But they are as a whole diffuse, chronologically vague, repetitive, and stuffed with bombast and digression. Many notable names went uncelebrated. Not one is about Kitty Clive. Foote is neglected, as are G. F. Cooke, Nell Gwynn, the Giffards, the Hallams.

As the nineteenth century wore on, the plight of anyone interested in actors' lives worsened, as did the plight of serious students of every other aspect of theatre from the Restoration to the Regency. While a few brass-rubbing country parsons and village schoolmasters were producing their footling chronicles of local theatrical history, scarcely more sophisticated London folk were weaving together sentimental fantasies, risqué remembrances, and inaccurate and gap-filled stage careers to produce wan or contrivedly sensational "biography." (There were a few bright spots: R. W. Lowe was preparing for better days with his *Bibliographical Account of English Theatrical Literature* and Joseph Knight was writing the some hundreds of flawed but remarkably dependable short notices of performers for *The Dictionary of National Biography.*)

Nor can I honestly say much good about the early and middle twentieth century.[2] But in 1958 John Harold Wilson wrote *All the King's Ladies,* in an excellent exercise in multiple biography, demonstrating, among many other good things, how sound documentary scholarship may not harm—may, indeed, enhance—good juicy gossip. And we seem now also to be entering on an era in which book-length, full-dress, theatrical biography of figures from 1660 to 1800 will be soundly and interestingly produced. One need only cite William Appleton's recent life of Macklin and Simon Trefman's new life of Foote; one need only anticipate Cecil Price's life of Sheridan, and Kahrl and Stone's life of Garrick.

I have drawn you into the thickets of bibliography only to show that making a dictionary of performers could not have been managed in any respectable way by relying to any *decisive* extent on previous biographies of performers, as valuable as those biographies certainly are.

We are sometimes asked, "Well, how *did* you start? Once you set out to do this odd thing, how did you know, beyond the first fifty or a hundred well-publicized names, even who the performers were?" The answer, of course, was "playbills," for this was before the days of *The London Stage 1660–1800.*[3] We did go to playbills by the thousands while we waited impatiently for the first volumes of that indispensable work. But the first encouragement to our enterprise was provided by Professor Stone and, a little later, by Professor Scouten, who generously turned over to me some thousands of names in their developing files. These constituted the stum without which our wine might never have fermented. These names, with their approximate dates, would lead to searches of parish registers and published sources of many kinds, and to wills in Somerset House, all of which would furnish death dates which would lead back again to wills and marriage and burial and baptismal registers which would suggest further relationships. (Much later in the process the late Emmett Avery gave us invaluable hand-indices of his volumes, and Beecher Hogan donated hundreds of biographical files of admirable accuracy.) Using the old Lowe bibliography, we went ahead to reading and stripping printed theatrical books, pamphlets, and poems, and still our name-file grew.

I had taught seventeenth- and eighteenth-century literature for some time and thought I knew where the small caches of literary reference to performance and social occurrence were: *The Tatler's* fun with Nicolini, Pepys's flirtation with "dear Knepp"; Boswell's affair with "Lavinia," Mrs. Cowper; Pope's deft skewering of Cibber; Walpole's admiration for Kitty Clive; Fielding's description of the effect of Garrick's Hamlet on Partridge; Lamb's commendation of Munden; Aaron Hill's apt characterization of Jemmy Quin as "Mr. Allweight," James Thomson's compliment to him as the "Aesopus of the Age," and Smollett's attacks on him in *Humphry Clinker;* Davies's introduction of Boswell to Johnson, and so on. But not only did all of the works of all the poets, playwrights, and novelists have to be inspected, so also did news-paper squibs, broadside ballads, epitaphs; not only did literary and stage biography have to be reviewed, so also did all *likely* biography, memoirs, and letters, published and unpublished, from the manuscript diary of Tom King to James Winston's transcripts of letters of Kitty Clive, from the chaste and genteel *Journals and Letters of Fanny Burney*[4] to the steamy reminiscences of the rake-hell William Hickey.[5]

At Somerset House in 1960 the stack men refused to bring up more than six volumes of wills for inspection each day, and I had by then already accumulated many hundreds of firm death dates to investigate. So I took wing some thousands of miles westward to Salt Lake City, where the hospitable Mormons had on film all the British wills from 1384. Information on middling and small musicians was in short supply. So Kalman Burnim persuaded the Royal Society of Musicians for the first time to open files on many hundreds of musicians, showing birth and death dates, baptisms, marital states, professional specialties, employment, children. Ed Langhans had joined the project, bringing with him his great hoard of seventeenth-century minutiae. One or another of us settled for weeks or months at the Huntington, the British Museum, the Harvard Theatre Collection, the Public Record Office, the national archives of Scotland and Ireland, the Bibliothèque Nationale, the Enthoven Collection, wherever there were manuscripts. At each repository we read manuscripts until they were exhausted, then turned to early printed books unavailable elsewhere. Always new leads were turning up new death dates, sending us back to parish registers, back to wills, which again produced further spiderwebs of relationship of marriage and liaison, bastardy and business.

We have our humble tales of luck and suspense and serendipity and shrewdness. If we can seldom match in complication and fascination those recently told by James Clifford in *From Puzzles to Portraits,* it is because we were not at most points digging deeper and deeper into the life of any one individual. Instead of much such "vertical" biography, involving intense concentration on one person, we were, generally,

41

doing "horizontal" research, strip-mining, if you like, and gathering in everything about everybody at once. We proceeded roughly chronologically, but we filed alphabetically; and since we were also to publish alphabetically, virtually *all* research had to be done before the first entry could be written. This gave us years of leisure to sort, cross-index, ponder and wonder, bring complicated relationships clear, and, finally, for some individuals and to a limited extent, go back and try some of the vertical research we had in the first instance eschewed. All that sounds dreadfully unplanned, and it was. There was only a slowly developing pattern, for we had no precedent. But more and more performers' names emerged as we read more bills, saw more of the volumes of *The London Stage* come out. And though at first and for a long time there was precious little justification for faith, we believed that we could find out a great many facts about these obscure people. Over the years we followed that conviction to more than sixty libraries and muniment rooms.

There were disappointments, of course, like my grandiose scheme of working with the manuscript parish registers of City churches in the London Guildhall. I would simply draw a ring around the theatrical districts of each period and, employing contemporaneous maps which indicated parish boundaries, close the ring until I began turning up theatrical people in the registers. The scheme was abandoned after wasted weeks, because of the undependability of parish clerks, most of whom failed to distinguish parishioners' professions. We have had to content ourselves largely with the rich ore from registers of a few known theatrical churches, most of which have been printed by the Harleian Society: especially St. Paul, Covent Garden, but also St. Paul's Cathedral, Westminster Abbey, St. Martin-in-the-Fields, St. Giles in the Fields, St. Marylebone, St. George, Hanover Square, and so on. Sometimes, when we could locate families, we did intensive searches in manuscript registers in and out of London.

My generation was taught by its mentors in graduate school that one should maintain an attitude of stoic reticence concerning the difficulties attending a work. And it is not from

42

any vainglorious notion that we were singled out by the baneful Fates for special trials that I now turn to the enumeration of some problems. On the contrary, without falling over into hubris—for the work is far from finished—we feel that we have been especially fortunate.

I will list a few problems, just as they come to mind, to show the variety, though I can only suggest the number: first of all, and repeatedly, the problem of how to raise large sums of money for released time, travel, supplies, secretarial help. How far should we go over into exposition of a marginally theatrical person's second profession? What are our responsibilities toward continental, provincial, American, and nineteenth-century careers? How far down in time would we trace individual genealogy when it was available? For instance, the Minute Books of the Royal Society of Musicians, relatively unexploited, often tell not only hard facts—birth, death, instrumental specialty—about a musician but also about his children and grandchildren. The rationalizations my colleagues and I have given each other sometimes for writing up this extended material have been ingenious, perhaps sometimes ingenuous: someone, somewhere, may be able to use these facts; or biographical information about the subject's widow and children is, after all, biographical information about the subject; or having received *some* information about a subject from the Minute Books, the reader will suppose he is being given all of it.

Some more problems: Should we include all roles played or only a selection—and then, alphabetical or chronological lists? How can we keep from darting too often down inviting scholarly rabbit-holes, writing articles and notes about the hundreds of interesting matters thrown up by our reading: heat and light, scenes and machines, management and direction, costuming, amateur theatricals, checks and bills, concessionaires, acting styles, foreigners, strolling companies? How would we handle, diplomatically and usefully, increasing streams of questions which come to the Folger from scholars who have heard—correctly—that our files are open? How were we to locate some 1800 pictures, identify their subjects, ascertain their provenance and history, correctly attribute them, obtain permissions, photograph and caption each? What were we to do about inevitable *addenda* and *corrigenda,* about unpublished parish registers? There was the logistical problem of moving files and families for years or months from the British Museum to Salt Lake City to Boston; the perplexity of writing two volumes, while editing two more, while proofing two more, over a period of perhaps eight years; and the multifarious gnat-like frustrations which buzz about all editing and proofing, increased in mass theatrical biography by the complexities of varying headnotes and changing type-fonts and odd orthography and foreign testimony and numerous numbers: the 1759 which comes out 1795 and, corrected, then turns up as 1975; or at *last* finding a printer who can handle the spelling of Aldiborontiphoscophornio, but who fouls up that character's play, *Chrononhotonthologos.*

But let me select and explore one or two problems much larger than that of myopic printers. One of the most vexatious problems was deciding whom to include in the *Dictionary.* We got no help from other biography. Already separated in form and technique from book-length one-person biography, our work was isolated also from every other sort of biographical dictionary both by its confinement to one profession in one period and our insistence on comprehensiveness within that profession. We are *sui generis,* for the *Dictionary of National Biography, Biographie Universelle,* and so on, cast wider nets, embracing all times and professions. On the other hand, to employ Dr. Johnson's definition of "network," our reticulation is decussated with narrower interstices between the intersections, so that we catch very small fish as well as the largest ones. Whereas the *DNB* seems interested in only the more considerable creatures, we democratically insist that even the least of the theatrical odd fish who made the varied shows of 1660 to 1800 so fascinating deserve to be caught.

We aimed, to quote the Preface to our volumes, "to provide brief biographical notices of all persons who were members of theatrical companies or occasional performers or were patentees or servants of the patent theatres, opera houses, amphitheatres, pleasure gardens, theatrical taverns, music rooms, fair booths, and other places of public entertainment in London and its immediate environs from the Restoration . . . until the end of the season 1799–1800." But of course our Preface was written calmly after the fact. And that large—some have said suicidal—inclusiveness was the product of much mind-struggle. Actors we naturally began with, singers and dancers followed as naturally; managers, prompters, of course, then instrumentalists. But funambulists, sibilists, pyrotechnists, posture-makers, equestrians? Scene shifters, callers, wigmakers, clowns to the ring, doorkeepers, treasurers, carpenters? Our difficulty was twofold: first, we began to develop a certain breadth and tolerance in our definitions of worthy entertainment and estimable entertainer, a feeling for the total performance which Dean Stone has told us Garrick possessed and that certainly the audience had; second, there was the difficulty of determining whether or not some musicians were "theatrical."

The world of entertainment was large. *The London Stage* lists a total, for the entire 140 years of our purview, of some 240 *locations* of paid entertainment in London. We add perhaps 20 more. But even that total of about 260 for the period probably falls short of the truth. Let me illustrate how the audiences of the day looked at the world of "entertainment." The first Duchess of Northumberland remarked to her diary in 1773: "There was certainly no deficiency or want of public amusements this Year for I can enumerate the following Theatres, Concerts, Wells, Spas, Pleasure gardens, and various other Places of Entertainment." And enumerate she does, to the number of 78, leading off with "Drury Lane, Covent Garden, Lesser Haymarket, Opera Houses" but then going directly to "Strollers at Bow, Do. in Borough . . . Sadlers Wells, Bagnigge, Battle Bridge, Dog & Duck, Islington." Cheek-by-jowl and higgledy-piggledy she lists Vaux Hall, the Pantheon, various ridottos, George Alexander Stevens's Lecture on Heads, Sheridan's "Oratory," Behiron's anatomical figures, "Bachs Concert, Giardinis," the Royal Society, "Billiard Tables & Cockpits," and Salmon's waxworks—"besides Wild Beasts in every Street in Town."[6]

Such catholicity of taste among the aristocracy may have been unusual, but not everyone was as fastidious as Horace Walpole. Carnevale, himself a person of some consequence at the Italian Opera, established a *fantoccini* theatre by hiring the painter Biaggio Rebecca to prank out Squibb's Auction Room with "arabesque paintings." Rebecca had been helping the architect of the Pantheon, James Wyatt, decorate lordly Heaton Hall in Manchester and Hevingham Hall in Suffolk, and he was sometimes employed to paint scenes for Drury Lane Theatre. The audience at the marionettes included the Duke of Bedford, the Duke of Cumberland, Lord Salisbury, Lord Cadogan, and Lord Cholmondeley.[7] Impresario, artist, and audience all understood the *fantoccini* to be valid *entertainment.*

Under our definition, many of our folk could have entered these volumes under any of several specialties. They were all *entertainers,* perhaps more than in any other century dedicated to the total effect of the bill. Many could not afford (nor cared) to stick closely to one specialty. Singers acted, actors danced, dancers sang. They learned variousness in country companies and sometimes in London. The young Thomas John Dibdin, by the time he was twenty-one, could, as he boasted, "sing 'Poor Jack,' paint scenes, play the fiddle, write a farce, get up a pantomime, attempt Sir Francis Gripe, Apollo in 'Midas,' Mungo in the 'Padlock,' Darby in the 'Poor Soldier,' Captain Valentine in the 'Farmer,' and Polonius in 'Hamlet;' not to mention all dialects, as the Irishman in 'Rosina,' or anything else, with French and German characters . . ."[8] A little later he learned to prompt and to manage. James Thomas Kirkman says of the young Charles Macklin as an itinerant:

It would be an uninteresting and tiresome task to the reader to go through . . . the various characters he played, or the variety of offices he executed. Sometimes he was an architect, and knocked up the stage and seats in a barn; sometimes he wrote an opening

46

Prologue, or a parting Epilogue, for the company: at others, he wrote a song, complimentary and adulatory to the village they happened to play in, which he always adapted to some sprightly popular air, and sung himself: and he often was champion and stood forward to repress the persons who were accustomed to intrude upon, and be rude to the actors.[9]

Later, between fights, feuds, litigations, duels, and successes as a tragic actor, Macklin managed, gave lessons in acting and elocution, was a successful playwright, and lectured in his oratory.

But other inclusions were not so easy. Even folk with more than one string to their bows (or, in the case of several we are about to mention, more than one bow for their strings) stood uncertainly on the periphery of the "theatrical" circle. We had to determine theatrical persons by performance and professionals by pay. But location had something to do with the matter, too, especially when musicians were concerned. Was a given performance in a church, at Court, in a private home, in a theatre, in a tavern? Were the Handelian memorial performances of sacred oratorio in Westminster Abbey in May and June 1784 theatrical performances? Perhaps not, although the musicians were paid. But the festival moved on alternate days to the secular Pantheon, and admission was charged. Are the many provincial musicians employed for those performances (and who never performed anywhere else in London) *London* performers? After argument, we included all of them, preferring to stretch the meanings of "professional," "London," and even "theatrical," rather than to chance leaving someone out who should be in.

Sticking to music (and moving from one end to the other of our chronological span), as William Bingley observed in his *Musical Biography* (1814): "All the most eminent composers for the theatre, for several years after the Restoration, were members of cathedral and collegiate churches: this circumstance occasioned Tom Brown to say, that 'men of the musical profession hung betwixt the church and the playhouse, like Mahomet's tomb betwixt two loadstones.' "[10] To an author of musical biography Brown's *mot* was simply a clever quote.

To the authors of a biographical dictionary of *all* professional theatrical people the saying bites deep. Again, in the matter of the Gentlemen of the Chapel Royal, we waffle a bit in our Preface:

> We have provided information about several hundred Restoration Court musicians, most of whom are not recorded in *Grove's Dictionary of Music and Musicians*. There is ample proof that some of these people also performed, usually with (but occasionally without) royal permission, at public concerts and theatres; but for many we find no certain evidence of performances away from the Court. Rather than consign these partially documented musicians to oblivion, we have included them, hoping that future research will bear out our conjecture that most Court employees, because their wages were so often in arrears, sought supplementary employment.

There were reasons for admitting tradesmen salaried at the theatres—barbers, carpenters, and so on—besides their right to be included because their contributions were valuable. Their social ties with performers were often close, and they were often commercially important, thus turning up often in the correspondence of the period and hence requiring identification. And then, again, there was our commitment to completeness. Our house servants—boxkeepers, under treasurers, and the like—were solidly important to the welfare of the theatre, and their benefit receipts demonstrate the assiduity with which they kept in touch with the town. Sometimes, also, they doubled in performance. I cite John Claridge, lobby doorkeeper, who, according to the Folger's Drury Lane account books, alternated with John Doe and others in the season of 1771–72 playing in "the Ass and Hog"—that is to say, stuffing himself into the animated properties in the pantomime *Mother Shipton*. Not really good parts, perhaps, but necessary, if anonymous.

Admittedly, some of our people *are* marginal or dubious. Joseph ("Proteus") Clark, the posture-maker, amazed the town with his contortions. Of him Evelyn wrote in his *Numismata* (1667) that he "was of so flexible and subtile a Texture, as to contort his Members into several disfigurations, and to put out of joynt almost any Bone or *Vertebra* of his Body, and to re-place it again."[11] There is no documentary proof from bills, payments, or references that Clark exhibited for pay. But the drawings by Marcellus Laroon in Tempest's *Cries of London* (1711) showing Clark's contortions are persuasive of his professionalism.

Regretfully, we had to draw the line before sword-fighters and pugilists, colorful as their challenges and gory as their battles were, unless they formed a subsidiary part of a real theatrical bill. Hear this challenge and response, quoted in a *London Journal* of June 1722:

> I Elizabeth Wilkinson, of Clerkenwell, having had some words with Hannah Hyfield, and requiring satisfaction, do invite her to meet me on the Stage, and box with me for three guineas, each woman holding half a crown in each hand, and the first woman that drops her money to lose the battle.
>
> I Hannah Hyfield, of Newgate-market, hearing of the resoluteness of Elizabeth Wilkinson, will not fail, [God] willing, to give her more blows than words, desiring home blows, and from her no favour.

A fashion note: the combatants were habited in "close jackets, short petticoats, Holland drawers, white stockings, and pumps." Sadly, Hannah Hyfield and Elizabeth Wilkinson are lost to history until someone does the definitive dictionary of pugilism. We have, however, another Miss Wilkinson, Isabella, who sails into our volumes on multiple wings of talent: daring slack-wire walker, she could also sing, dance, and play upon the violin, harpsichord, and musical glasses.

Let me speak now a little bit about inclusion of a different sort—about what is admissible as evidence. To recur to our Preface:

> Like all biographers and historians, we have placed greatest reliance on firsthand factual evidence, particularly from any legal or quasi-legal *locus:* sworn courtroom testimony, legal depositions, wills, parish registers, and theatrical account books. Nearly as credible are diaries, letters, and annotated playbills. Epitaphs are fairly trustworthy, and so is necrology published in periodicals soon after the event (though occasionally we find actors indignantly correcting reports of their deaths). Somewhat murkier are the memoirs. In employing these we have had to make a careful analysis of motive

and wide allowance for the vagaries of aging memory before granting credence. In every critique of performance the possibility of bias has been considered, particularly if the criticism was current—for, if encomiastic, it may have been a puff written or inspired by an interested manager, or, if pejorative, a libel paid for by a jealous rival.

"Well," you may say, "all that is obvious, just common sense." But the ranking is not invariable. We know of perjured courtroom testimony and dishonest depositions. Letters can be faked and altered. Attitudes in diaries can be feigned and often are. Let me illustrate the grounds of my skepticism. We are accustomed to believe that manuscript salary lists in theatrical accounts of the eighteenth century are as good as gold. Almost always they are. But even here one can pan fool's gold. After Giovanni Andrea Battista Gallini (commonly called "Sir John") had acquired control of the opera at the King's Theatre in 1784, he was required by a suspicious Lord Chamberlain to furnish security, to appoint a receiver-treasurer, and to certify the amounts he proposed to pay his performers. He answered all three requirements. But a letter dated 17 November 1785 from Gallini to the Lord Chamberlain survives in the Public Record Office to warn us just how deceptive even documents deposed to legal authority *may* be. Gallini writes that he had sent his Lordship copies of

the different contracts I had entered into with the Performers as the same were signed by me, and among the rest Signora Ferrarese's which is made for £650 as your Lordship was informed by me, purposely to prevent her losing her credit in Italy should it be known she had engaged for so small a sum as £500 which I am to give her and no more, and which I likewise mentioned to your Lordship. I should esteem it a very material honor . . . not to let it be revealed as I should be very unwilling either to prejudice her here or abroad, but being determin'd to act with the utmost Candour by your Lordship I conceived it right to apprise you how the Affair stood; the rest are to be paid as their Contracts specify . . .

Gallini adds, significantly, "it is customary with some to enter into Agreements for a greater Amount than they are to receive in order not to hurt their reputation abroad." Customary?

50

The questions naturally arise: "Are many opera salary lists honeycombed with this deceit? Does the practice ever extend from those devious and mendacious Italians at the Opera to honest John Bull at the legitimate drama houses? How came the Lord Chamberlain into such collusion?"

Playbills are the most numerous pieces of surviving evidence about many matters: roles and persons, specialties like singing and dancing. But also: street addresses on benefit bills, printers' names, prices, times of performance, heating and lighting, set design, choreography, command performances, advertising practices, and so on and on right down to paper and watermarks. We have had to depend a great deal on playbills, not only Dr. Stone and colleagues' reports of London bills, but on kinds of London bills which we collected and which they did not, and on a great many continental, Irish, Scottish, English provincial, and American bills.

But bills can also be cruelly deceptive. Sometimes when they proclaim that a younger performer in London is appearing "for the first time on any stage," the ostensible novice has already been seasoned for a considerable period on provincial stages and is being introduced in this way so that the newspaper writers and the Dick Minims of the town will cry up the natural ability of the prodigy. (On the other hand, it sometimes better suited a manager's purposes to introduce a provincial youngster of limited experience or talent after a careful campaign of paid puffery in the newspapers.)

There is plenty of evidence of the fallibility of bills—last-minute changes, for instance, of everything from cast to afterpiece, misspelling, misdating. Let me give just one instance of many which could be cited illustrating change of fare. This one amusingly combines several typical difficulties. The journal quoted is the *True Briton* for 13 January 1796:

The representation announced for last night at this Theatre was *Twelfth Night;* but as Mrs. Jordan found herself too ill to perform, new bills were issued, and the substitute was to be *The Siege of Belgrade.* About the middle of the day, however, Mrs. Jordan found herself well enough to perform, and the other bills were circulated, importing that the play was to be *Twelfth Night.* But, in the afternoon,

Mrs. Jordan found herself too ill to perform, and a message was sent again to the theatre, signifying the melancholy disappointment. It was then too late to make any other change, and *Twelfth Night* was represented, Mrs. Goodall reading the part of Viola. There was considerable difficulty in collecting the performers, after these repeated changes. Barrymore could not be found, and Caulfield dressed for Orsino; but when he was ready to appear Barrymore arrived, and took the part. It was then discovered that Phillimore was absent, and Caulfield was doomed to dress once more, for Phillimore's character; but soon after Phillimore came to the house. Mrs. Kemble being indisposed, Miss Mellon undertook her part of Maria . . . The Audience (a large one) indeed grumbled a little at this kind of dramatic *hocus pocus,* but on the whole, were not churlish . . .[12]

Though an extreme example, this kind of thing was by no means infrequent; it was not always reported in the press; and the authors of *The London Stage* and the *Biographical Dictionary* are to expect—for the rest of our lives, perhaps—little notes in *Notes & Queries* or the *Times Literary Supplement* triumphantly correcting our bill-based assertions and citing some late resurrection of a playgoer's diary or manager's letter.

I could weary you with citation, for there are soft spots in every *source* of evidence—even in wills, even in parish registers. But by all odds the toughest and most constant challenge to the integrity and accuracy of mass biography—and I would claim especially to mass theatrical biography—comes from a *kind* of evidence found in several *sources* of evidence. I speak now of anecdote—anecdote, which is impossible to resist using if one aspires, in Thomas Fuller's words, "to entertain the reader with delight" and to make him depart *jocundior* as well as *doctior,* or, to hark to an earlier and even more eminent master, to furnish the *dulce* as well as the *utile.* Joseph Haslewood, in his anonymously-published *Secret History of the Green Room Containing Authentic and Entertaining Memoirs of the Actors and Actresses of the Three Theatres Royal,* says in the preface to his second edition (1792):

The avidity with which Anecdote is sought, of those who have in any path attained eminence, is one of the most general and natural propensities of mankind. Of this passion, to which the Biographer of Sages and Heroes ministers, it is our humble province to attempt the gratification by becoming the Historians of the Sons and Daughters of the Buskin, which will, we trust, prove *"not a less pleasing, though a less glorious theme."*

Because it indeed bulks so large, and is so troublesome and so fascinating, I want to spend most of the rest of my time wrestling the problem of anecdotal evidence.

It is impossible to walk in Paul's Churchyard and not think (if one knows the story) of the eminent musician Jeremiah Clarke, who shot himself there. A story exists that, in an earlier fit of melancholy, he had flipped a coin to decide whether to commit suicide by hanging or by drowning and that it had landed in the mud and stuck, upright. That had decided him to live a little longer.[13] We reported the story, but I trust in a manner to indicate our mistrust. George Colman the younger, in his *Random Records* (a title whose two halves reflect about equally the volume's constituent parts), was a considerable retailer of colorful fabrications. His longer anecdotes are not so insidious, however, as his occasional biographical tidbit, calculated to make the antiquary perk up his ears. For example: "Mr. James Dance, much better known as Mr. Love . . . a translation of his wife's maiden name of *De L'Amour.*"[14] How fortunate that we *know* that Dance's wife was the daughter of James Hooper, and that Dance had settled on Love as his stage name before he met her.[15]

Burney reports that the Italian male contralto singer Carestini sent the song "Verdi prati," from *Alcina,* back to its composer, Handel, as not suited to Carestini's style. Handel rushed to the singer's house, shouting, "You tog! don't I know petter as yourseluf vaat es pest for you to sing? If you vill not sing all de song vaat I give you, I vill not pay you ein stiver." The story is obviously apocryphal. Why, then, did Burney, usually shrewd and truthful, repeat it? And why did Julian Marshall tell it again in *Grove's Dictionary,* even though he felt obliged to footnote his incredulity that Carestini knew English and that Handel didn't know Italian? The answer,

53

equally obvious, is the important principle often at work in anecdote-mongering: it is so *like* Handel—so like him that it has caught on, and must be told in order to refute it. So while we refute it we use it. Do we also perpetuate it?

John Williams, that notorious "Anthony Pasquin" whose privity to authentic theatrical scandal was equaled only by his lack of veracity, in his *The Pin-Basket to The Children of Thespis* (1797) tells one anecdote, perfectly convincing and no doubt true, of the prowess of the Drury Lane harlequin William Phillips. It involves a miraculous escape from death after one of Phillips's leaps, when his assistant failed to catch him. But Williams could scarcely ever leave well enough alone. He must continue with another story: Phillips "was a dissipated *bon vivant,* and much given to the interests of the Paphian Governess. One evening that his Majesty was to grace the Stage box, with a command for a favourite Pantomime, the Harlequin was not to be found . . ." The "well-scented hounds of the Theatre were dispatched in search of him" and finally found him. But bailiffs were gathered by the stage-door to arrest him, as was usually the case. They had to be hoodwinked. So "to effect this he was placed in a hamper, and a wine-porter carried him, as he was rolled up like a wood-louse (for he was small, and had been used to contract himself when a Tumbler, into little compass), in which state he passed safe through a congregation of bailiffs."[16] What would be your judgment on the use of this story? Did it happen? Or is Williams simply adopting and adapting his memories of Falstaff in *The Merry Wives of Windsor?* Or is he drawing on his knowledge of a harlequin-trick used not only in eighteenth-century pantomime but for ages back? *The Festival of Wit* (1806), a decade further removed from Harlequin Phillips than Williams was, reported that once Phillips was taken up for suspicion of debt, duped the bailiff at the sponging house into allowing him to send for a hamper of wine, and escaped in the hamper on the porter's back.[17] Is this a variant only? Can Phillips have done this thing habitually, bringing professional expertise often to the service of his well-known dissoluteness? Was his art repeatedly instructing his life?

Anecdote is an apt, colorful, well-told story, somehow illustrative of character. The annalist looking for color can find plenty of verifiable anecdotes. He can fashion his own from the melancholy facts of wills. Giuseppe Grimaldi, for instance, bade his daughter Mary make personally certain that he would be beheaded before his burial, so strong was his fear of being buried alive[18]—a grim coda to the life of the father of perhaps the greatest clown who ever lived. The facts were not, however, developed to the point of anecdote by the retailers of the early Grimaldi stories, probably because they had not seen his will.

Speaking of heads, a thorough illustration of the difficulty either of accepting or of rejecting some lurid legends has been furnished recently by Don B. Wilmeth in the matter of the allegedly misplaced skull of George Frederick Cooke. For years after that dipsomaniac thespian genius was buried in St. Paul's churchyard in New York in 1812, stories floated concerning the partial dismemberment of his body. In 1832 the painter-manager William Dunlap wrote, cryptically, "it may hereafter be found that his surgeon possesses his scull, and his successor, Kean, the bones of the forefinger of his right-hand,—that dictatorial finger,—still the monument covers the *remains* of George Frederick Cooke." There was talk that the skull had been loaned out for the fifth act of *Hamlet*. The story had seemed Gothically incredible for this skeptical age. But Wilmeth demonstrated its essential truth and even added embellishments. The skull had indeed been taken by Dr. V. M. Francis, one of the physicians who had attended Cooke at his last illness, but only in 1821, when Cooke's body was exhumed and buried in another part of the churchyard. Francis in time passed the skull on to his son, who gave it to the Dean of the Jefferson Medical College in Philadelphia, where it is displayed today. On one occasion Dr. Francis did actually lend the skull for a production of *Hamlet*. Moreover, a tooth was sent to Edwin Booth, who gave it to the Player's Club. It is now in the City Museum of New York. Alas, nothing is known of the dictatorial forefinger.[19]

I prefer less macabre anecdote. So did Thomas Davies. But

55

dare we hope that the following pleasant story is veritable? Davies relates that Colley Cibber, in his first appearance onstage, was a messenger, supposed to be carrying a note to the leading actor Thomas Betterton. When Cibber saw the audience he panicked and botched the scene. After the play, Betterton asked Downes the prompter who the awkward youngster was. "Master Colley," said Downes. "Master Colley! then forfeit him." "Why, sir," said Downes, "he has no salary." "No! Why then put him down ten shillings a week and forfeit him 5s."[20]

How much more—or less—credible is a story whose subject is also its recounter? In 1775 the four-year-old Thomas John Dibdin and his brother Charles were allowed to march in the procession of characters in a revival of the Shakespearean spectacle *The Jubilee,* at Drury Lane. Thomas, "an extraordinarily beautiful boy," he says, was selected for the Cupid to walk hand-in-hand with Mrs. Siddons, who walked as Venus. One of his wings dropped off and Mrs. Siddons borrowed a pin from Garrick's servant to re-attach it. "I recollect," says Dibdin, "that at the nightly conclusion of the Jubilee, tarts, cheesecakes, and other pastry were very liberally distributed to the juvenile corps, who personated the fairies, &c. . . . and Mr. Garrick himself . . . stayed, for the pleasure he felt in witnessing a due distribution of said bonbons."[21] How charming: the avuncular Garrick, the lovely children, the heavenly queenly Siddons, and that marvelous touch, the pinning-on of the fallen wing. But how exact is it all? Certainly that season *The Jubilee* was revived, though in none of its thirty-four bills is there a cast. But Dibdin is harking back from the year 1827. How many of us can remember for fifty-two years details occurring when we were age four?

An example of eminently believable and certainly affecting anecdote was published in the *Public Advertiser* of 5 February 1784, reporting the performance of 29 January 1784 at Covent Garden and illustrating that, in the writer's words, "If Macklin once loses the Catch Word he is gone irretrievably." Charles Macklin was at least eighty-four years old, and failing in all of his powers. And, notwithstanding that he was playing Sir

Pertinax Macsycophant in his own play *The Man of the World,* the account says that when some apprentices came into the pit and talked loudly "Macklin stopped; he lost himself . . . He came to the Side of the Stage, and stooping down to the Talkers, said, 'Gentlemen, I must beg you to be silent; my Hearing and recollection are not so perfect as they were: I cannot proceed for your Talking." The pathetic vignette shows better than a chapter what Macklin had declined to at this hour of his life, and published immediately after the performance, it is likely to have been accurate, or it would not have stood the test of refutation by hundreds of auditors.

Similarly revealing and just as credible was the story given by the *Public Advertiser* in reporting a Covent Garden performance of 4 November 1778: "In speaking a line in the Prologue that won applause Whitfield waved his hat so vehemently that he dislocated a Bone in his Arm. He went to the side of the stage, and one of the Scene-men taking him by the Wrist, and giving four or five pretty severe jerks, the Bone recovered its place." And the show went on.

Everyone is familiar with the mistaken supposition by Shelley[22] before he wrote *Adonais* that an anonymous 1818 article in the *Quarterly Review* which had been written by John Wilson Croker was one of three reviews of *Endymion* which had hastened the death of John Keats. That notion is now all but universally rejected. Curiously, we learn now that fourteen years earlier, in 1804, the same J. W. Croker had published *Familiar Epistles,* a poetic satire on the performers of the Dublin stage which created a local furore and gave rise to similar charges. In it, Croker called the comedian John Edwin, Jr., the "lubbard spouse" of Mrs. Edwin and compared him unfavorably with his father. Upon reading the lines, Edwin is supposed to have written to a friend: "Come and help me to destroy myself with some of the most splendid cogniac [*sic*] that I have ever exported to cheer a broken heart." Everything we know about Edwin would suggest that the lines were jocular. And we also know that he had already enthusiastically followed the bibulous example of his father. Would he not have drunk himself to death without the stimulation

57

of a satire? Are not then the rumors that he did so because of the satire romantic? One would have said so. Yet his wife Elizabeth Rebecca caused the following lines to be incised on his tombstone in St. Werburgh's churchyard, Dublin:

Here lie the remains of Mr. JOHN EDWIN, of the Theatre-Royal, who died Feb. 22, 1805, aged 33 years. His death was occasioned by the acuteness of his sensibility [Ah! the power of that word in 1805!]. Before he was sufficiently known to the public of this city, to have his talents properly appreciated, he experienced an illiberal and cruel attack on his professional reputation, from an anonymous assassin. This circumstance preyed upon his mind to the extinction of life.

While in apparent bodily vigour, he predicted his approaching dissolution. The consciousness of a brain rending with agony, accounts for this prescience, and incontrovertibly establishes the cause of his death.[23]

Are actors more sensitive than poets? Or just harder drinkers? One is reminded of the charge, repeated in 1771 by Francis Gentleman in *The Theatres* and in 1772 by David Williams,[24] that Garrick, by mimicking Dennis Delane (in 1748), had had "such an effect on the mind of poor Delane," in Williams's words, ". . . that it absolutely occasioned his death." Gentleman had said that "having generous, though week [*sic*] feelings, Mr. Delane took to drinking, and in reality broke his heart."[25]

So, credibility is seldom certain. But then neither is incredibility. Virtually the identical anecdote is told of the tutelage of Carlo Broschi (the great castrato called Farinelli) and of Gaetano Maiorano (called Caffarelli). Both were students of the great Porpora. After singing the two notes F and B—and no more—for three years, and after two years of practicing the trill, and then two more singing before a looking glass, Farinelli came humbly to his master and asked, "Master, what more shall I do to attain perfection?" Porpora replied, "Go, my son; you have no further need of me. You are the greatest singer in the world."[26] After virtually the same discipline, Cafarelli asked much the same question, and was told, "Go, my son: I have nothing more to teach you. You are the greatest

58

singer in Europe."[27] Which of the lads did Porpora tell this to? Both? Neither? Was it a sort of graduation citation which he gave to all of his pupils?

Are we to believe that poor, illegitimate John Davy when he was six years old stole twenty or thirty horseshoes from the village farrier and, when apprehended, had selected eight to form an octave and "had suspended each of them by a single cord . . . and, with a small iron rod, was amusing himself by imitating the Crediton [church] chimes which he did with great exactness"?[28] Does not this smack a little of the tale attached to several great musicians about an infant prodigy creeping downstairs to resolve the unresolved chord on the pianoforte? But might not *all* these stories be true? After all, what more colorfully unlikely than that Tom Dogget should have left funds by his will to ensure that the Thames watermen should row each year, down to this present, for a fine coat and a silver badge? But they do, they do. Or that Robert Baddeley should have provided by his will cake and wine down to this very month, for actors in the green room of Drury Lane theatre on Twelfth Night. But he did.

I will close this brief excursus into anecdote by retelling one oft told, but which I consider the quintessential exemplar from every point of view—being of credible source and a wonderful illustration of the characters involved and an excellent example of that repartee which the wittiest of centuries delighted in. In a letter of 23 January 1742, the Countess of Hertford wrote:

About ten days ago Mrs. Woffington and Mrs. Clive met in the Green Room. Mrs. Woffington came up to Mrs. Clive and told her she had long looked for the favor of a visit from her and that she begged she would let her know when she designed her that pleasure, for she was often engaged in an afternoon. Mrs. Clive paused a little and then answered, "Madam, I have been thinking of it, and upon consideration find I have a reputation to lose." "Madam," said Mrs. Woffington, "so should I have too if I had your face."[29]

No, anecdote is not just a condiment. It is part of the meat, and it may be for many readers the tastiest part of this mince-pie of *biographia collectanea*.

This whole matter of anecdote introduces now the question of the mass biographer's—any biographer's—twin responsibilities: (A) to the subject, though perhaps long dead, and (B) to the reader, though unknown, and in many cases unborn. Neither subject nor reader will ever know how true or false we have been to him. If they could know, surely the desire of each should be not only that the cause be reported aright but that at least something of the reality of each life should be suggested, where possible. But it is seldom possible to do *more* than suggest in a work whose entries range from one line to sixty pages, which serves only as a census for some figures but supplies near-monograph-length biographies for others. The biographer can seldom be more than a kind of spiritual taxidermist, even for the largest and most completely-realized figure. Any illusion that the figure moves is just that—illusion. Some biographers, of even the greatest single figures, are more like the restorers of dinosaurs from fragments of toes and tailbones. The fewer facts known, the freer the biographer to indulge his own wish about his subject, even to commit that worst heresy, reading biography into an artist's art, or out of it. We are spared that temptation, for, before the day of film and phonograph, the art of the performing artist was writ on water.

We must try, of course, to capture as much of each essence as possible, somewhat consoled for each comparative failure by the consciousness that no Augustine, no Rousseau, no Pepys has ever told it all, even about himself, that even Gibbon, writing his autobiography, tried six versions, that John Opie painted thirty-three self-portraits and was still dissatisfied. For we all seek, for some comical reason, to curry favor with those who come after us, and it is our right to do so. And that fact, too, tightens the biographer's responsibility to his subject. But the knowledge that we have so few and such uncertain estimates of our subjects' art throws us back the more on the "illuminating" anecdotes of their personal lives, their "characters." And just as anecdotes tend to accrue to the more colorful "characters," they tend also to concern one or two parts of each character—Macklin's violence, or Daly's, or Rich's syntax and love of his cats, Whitley's irascibility, Kemble's pride, Kean's lechery. How much are we entitled to dwell on the stinginess of a Garrick or a Clementi or the drunkenness of a G. F. Cooke, and how much "color" dare we conscientiously suppress in order to come somewhere within the compass of Othello's wistful standard, which biographers routinely aspire to and invariably fall short of: "Nothing extenuate,/ Nor set down aught in malice"?

We all seek, as I have said, to put our best foot forward toward posterity. Francis Gentleman, the soldier-actor-author-critic-elocutionist, whom Garrick called a "dirty, dedicating knave," thought of himself as a superior person, but Fortune's stepchild. He furnished a brief autobiographical preface to his comedy *The Modish Wife* in order, as he said, "to anticipate any biographical manufacturer, who might in future, as actor or author, gibbet me up to the view of posterity . . ." But Gentleman wrote that memoir a decade before his death, and he selected his events more carefully than did Pepys or Cibber. It remains for us, exactly two hundred years after he wrote in January 1775, to determine—very tentatively— that he was not so superior as he pretended nor so degraded as Garrick charged.

Having confessed the mechanical manner—though without scissors and paste—in which facts for our volumes were discovered and arranged, I may now seem pretentious if I speak of any preoccupation with "style" or "tone." Are such words possible in speaking of this humble drudgery? Well, we think that scrupulous application of some fundamental principles of writing might make as much difference in the end product as caution about accepting evidence does.

First, it seemed that in style and tone as much as in choice of matter we should do our best to liberate theatrical lives from sensationalism for its own sake. Then, we have tried to keep in mind that we are, after all, writing a reference work, which will be applied to for *fact* by many an editor of letters, diaries, memoirs, plays, novels, poetry, and many a writer of social history. Thus, we have proscribed both overt editorializing and the condescension which is implicit in irony.

61

We set out, as Gibbon said he did, to find "the middle tone, between a dull chronicle and a rhetorical declamation . . ." For us that goal has sometimes been rendered discouragingly ideal, on the one hand by faceless facts and dull career recitals in one kind of entry, and on the other hand by the quoted rodomontado of contemporary criticism. So, simply because we lacked materials, some entries have fallen into one or another of Gibbon's extremes. A few—a very few, we hope—alternate to both extremes.

Anyway, what Sheridan is supposed to have called "Gibbon's luminous page" is beyond us, and a workaday reference should not aspire to constant luminosity. Tom Moore said that Sheridan protested that he had really said "voluminous page." We have at least tried to avoid that in our compendious offerings. But, even though information ought not be stifled by elegant formulation, we have thought that the more substantial entries ought to be somewhat less stolid than a Bow Street police docket. One sure way to vivify dry fact is to quote, from letters, diaries, verse epistles, legal proceedings. But we are trying to be judicious, never selecting solely for "quaintness" if the result would be to falsify the total impression. As for our own prose, an honest tale speeds best plainly told. We have grounded most flights, "For works may have more wit than does them good,/ As bodies perish through excess of blood." Nor have we sought to provide a seamless garment of style. But it may be that something like Unamuno's conception of the progressive sanchification of Don Quixote and the progressive quixotification of Sancho Panza is happening to the three writers as we move from volume to volume. We are not yet one Mr. Spectator.

That we are having what seems to be a happy issue out of all our affliction has been due to good friends, indulgent families and colleagues, phenomenal luck, and the generosity of our universities, of many foundations, and of libraries like the Clark. But it has been due also to the fact that, whatever Johnson may have thought about players and joint stools, our subjects were worthwhile—important artistically, socially, and economically.

Despite the enormous variety of its meat and condiments, we hope that our pudding, unlike the one Winston Churchill sent back to the kitchen because it "lacked theme," has found its motif in the common commitment to *entertainment* which binds together 9,000 people of three dozen overlapping specialties operating over a span of 140 years. We hope it will be consumed with enjoyment and nourishment.

Notes

1. Philip H. Highfill, Jr., Kalman A. Burnim, and Edward A. Langhans, *A Biographical Dictionary of Actors, Actresses, Musicians, Dancers, Managers & Other Stage Personnel in London, 1660–1800* (Carbondale: Southern Illinois University Press, 1973-), 14 vols. in progress.

2. That is, so far as the period 1660–1800 is concerned. Theatrical biography of the earlier seventeenth century has been well served by Gerald Eades Bentley, *The Jacobean and Caroline Stage* (Oxford: Clarendon Press, 1941–1968), and Edwin Nungezer, *A Dictionary of Actors and of Other Persons Associated with the Public Representation of Plays in England Before 1642* (New Haven: Yale University Press, 1929).

3. *A Calendar of Plays, Entertainments & Afterpieces Together with Casts, Box-Receipts and Contemporary Comment Compiled from the Playbills, Newspapers and Theatrical Diaries of the Period,* edited with critical introductions by William Van Lennep, Emmett L. Avery, Arthur H. Scouten, George Winchester Stone, Jr., and Charles Beecher Hogan (Carbondale: Southern Illinois University Press, 1960–1968), 5 pts. in 11 vols.

4. Ed. Joyce Hemlow with Curtis D. Cecil and Althea Douglas (Oxford: Clarendon Press, 1972-).

5. *The Prodigal Rake,* ed. Peter Quennell (New York: Dutton, 1962).

6. *The Diaries of a Duchess, Extracts from the Diaries of the First Duchess of Northumberland* (1716–1776), ed. James Greig (London: Hodder and Stoughton, 1926).

7. See George Speaight, *The History of the English Puppet Theatre* (London: Harrap, 1955), p. 135.

8. *The Reminiscences of Thomas Dibdin,* 1827, I, 162–163.

9. *Memoirs of the Life of Charles Macklin, Esq.,* 1799, I, 59–60.

10. I, 181.

11. p. 277.

12. Quoted by C. B. Hogan, *The London Stage,* Pt. 5, 1822.

13. Kirkman, I, 52.

14. II, 63.

15. See Dorothy Stroud, *George Dance* (London: Faber and Faber, 1971), Appendix.

16. pp. 226–227.

17. I, 24.

18. In his will, signed 2 March 1788.

19. See "The Posthumous Career of George Frederick Cooke," *Theatre Notebook,* XIV (Winter, 1969–1970), 68–74, for the story and for photographs of the skull and the tooth.

20. *Dramatic Miscellanies,* 1785, III, 445.

21. *The Reminiscences of Thomas Dibdin,* I, 12–14. As Dean Stone reminds us, Mrs. Siddons's memory of the Jubilee revival was focused on different—though not contradictory—details. Her recollections, edited by William Van Lennep in 1942, show the apprehensive preoccupation of the young actress, just twenty, with Garrick's solicitous approval, which drew down on her the disapprobation of envious older actresses: "This gained me the malicious apellation [*sic*] of *Garrick's Venus* and the ladies who so kindly bestowed it on me, so determinedly rushed before me in the last scene, that had he not broken through them all, and brought us forward with his own hand, my little Cupid and my self, whose appointed situations were in the very front of the stage, might as well have been in the Island of Paphos at that moment." She does not recall her Cupid's name. *The Reminiscences of Sarah Siddons* (Cambridge: Widener Library, 1942), pp. 5–6.

22. And even by Byron in *Don Juan:*

> Strange that the mind, that very fiery particle,
> Should let itself be snuffed out by an article.

23. The *Monthly Mirror,* VII n.s. (March, 1810), 188.

24. In *A Letter to David Garrick, Esq., on his Conduct as Manager and Actor at Drury Lane,* pp. 10–11.

25. *Ibid.,* p. 8.

26. As told in an early nineteenth-century clipping laid into Huntington Library extra-illustrated 288749.

27. As recounted by Frank Walker in *Grove's Dictionary of Music and Musicians,* 5th edn., 1966.

28. Repeated by Gordon Goodwin in Davy's entry in the *DNB.* The ultimate source is *The Thespian Dictionary* (1802).

29. Helen Sard Hughes, *The Gentle Hertford her Life and Letters* (New York: Macmillan, 1940), pp. 236–237.

Members of the Seminar

Malcolm J. Abzug
Elizabeth Ball
Ron Barnes
Dorothy Charles
George Clarke
Mr. & Mrs. Frederick Combellack
Mr. & Mrs. William E. Conway
Jackson Cope
Edna C. Davis
Mr. & Mrs. Robert Dent
Mr. & Mrs. Robert Dougan
Mr. David F. Foxon
Mrs. Winifred Freese
Norman Fruman
Mary Isabel Fry
Joseph Fuchs
Henry Goodman
Mr. & Mrs. William Granert
Hugh J. Gray
George Guffey
Elisabeth Heisch
Philip H. Highfill, Jr.
Lucyle Hook
Mrs. Edwin H. Kaye
Ellen Kelly
Mr. & Mrs. Roy Kidman
Mary Klinger
Helene Koon
Mr. & Mrs. Robert P. Lang
Leo Lemay
Frank Lentricchia
Harry Levinson
Patrick McCloskey
Patricia McMurray
Mary R. Mahl

Mr. & Mrs. William Matthews
William Melnitz
Ada Nisbet
Maximillian E. Novak
Beverly J. Onley
James M. Osborn
Robert L. Peters
Mr. & Mrs. James Phillips
Jean Preston
Francis Reed
Virginia Renner
Mr. & Mrs. Ralph Rice
Ruth apRoberts
Alan Roper
George Rousseau
Edward Saslow
Alice Scoufos
Sean Shesgreen
James Siemon
Claude Simpson
John M. Steadman
Mr. & Mrs. George Winchester Stone, Jr.
Mr. & Mrs. H. T. Swedenberg, Jr.
Neady Taylor
Diana Thomas
Peter L. Thorslev, Jr.
Mr. & Mrs. Norman J. W. Thrower
Mr. & Mrs. Kent van den Berg
Mr. & Mrs. Robert Vosper
Brooke Whiting
Raymund F. Wood
Mr. & Mrs. Daniel H. Woodward
Clifford Wurfel
Suellen Zecchini

William Andrews Clark Memorial Library Seminar Papers

Editing Donne and Pope. 1952.
    Problems in the Editing of Donne's Sermons, by George R. Potter.
    Editorial Problems in Eighteenth Century Poetry, by John Butt.

Music and Literature in England in the Seventeenth and Eighteenth Centuries. 1953.
    *Poetry and Music in the Seventeenth Century, by James E. Phillips.
    *Some Aspects of Music and Literature in the Eighteenth Century, by Bertrand H. Bronson.

Restoration and Augustan Prose. 1956.
    *Restoration Prose, by James R. Sutherland.
    *The Ironic Tradition in Augustan Prose from Swift to Johnson, by Ian Watt.

Anglo-American Cultural Relations in the Seventeenth and Eighteenth Centuries. 1958.
    *The Puritans in Old and New England, by Leon Howard.
    William Byrd: Citizen of the Enlightenment, by Louis B. Wright.

The Beginnings of Autobiography in England, by James M. Osborn. 1959.

Scientific Literature in Sixteenth and Seventeenth Century England. 1961.
    English Medical Literature in the Sixteenth Century, by C. D. O'Malley.
    English Scientific Literature in the Seventeenth Century, by Rupert Hall.

Francis Bacon's Intellectual Milieu. A Paper delivered by Virgil K. Whitaker at a meeting at the Clark Library, 18 November 1961, celebrating the 400th anniversary of Bacon's birth.

Methods of Textual Editing, by Vinton A. Dearing. 1962.

The Dolphin in History. 1963.
    The History of the Dolphin, by Ashley Montagu.

Modern Whales, Dolphins, and Porpoises, as Challenges to Our Intelligence, by John C. Lilly.

Thomas Willis as a Physician, by Kenneth Dewhurst. 1964.

History of Botany. 1965.
Herbals, Their History and Significance, by George H. M. Lawrence.
A Plant Pathogen Views History, by Kenneth F. Baker.

Neo-Latin Poetry of the Sixteenth and Seventeenth Centuries. 1965.
Daniel Rogers: A Neo-Latin Link between the Pléiade and Sidney's 'Areopagus,' by James E. Phillips.
*Milton as a Latin Poet, by Don Cameron Allen.

Milton and Clarendon: Papers on Seventeenth-Century English Historiography. 1965.
Milton as Historian, by French R. Fogle.
Clarendon and the Practice of History, by H. R. Trevor-Roper.

Some Aspects of Seventeenth Century English Printing with Special Reference to Joseph Moxon, by Carey S. Bliss. 1965.

Homage to Yeats, 1865–1965. 1966.
Yeats and the Abbey Theatre, by Walter Starkie.
Women in Yeats's Poetry, by A. Norman Jeffares.

Alchemy and Chemistry in the Seventeenth Century. 1966.
Renaissance Chemistry and the Work of Robert Fludd, by Allen G. Debus.
Some Nonexistent Chemists of the Seventeenth Century, by Robert P. Multhauf.

The Uses of Irony. 1966.
*Daniel Defoe, by Maximillian E. Novak.
*Jonathan Swift, by Herbert J. Davis.

Bibliography. 1966.
Bibliography and Restoration Drama, by Fredson Bowers.
In Pursuit of American Fiction, by Lyle H. Wright.

Words to Music. 1967.
English Song and the Challenge of Italian Monody, by Vincent Duckles.
Sound and Sense in Purcell's 'Single Songs,' by Franklin B. Zimmerman.

John Dryden. 1967.
*Challenges to Dryden's Biographer, by Charles E. Ward.
*Challenges to Dryden's Editor, by H. T. Swedenberg.

Atoms, Blacksmiths, and Crystals. 1967.
The Texture of Matter as Viewed by Artisan, Philosopher, and

Scientist in the Seventeenth and Eighteenth Centuries, by Cyril Stanley Smith.

Snowflakes and the Constitution of Crystalline Matter, by John G. Burke.

Laplace as a Newtonian Scientist, by Roger Hahn. 1967.

Modern Fine Printing. 1968.

The Private Press: Its Essence and Recrudescence, by H. Richard Archer.

Tradition and Southern California Printers, by Ward Ritchie.

Medical Investigation in Seventeenth Century England. 1968.

Embryological Thought in Seventeenth Century England, by Charles W. Bodemer.

Robert Boyle as an Amateur Physician, by Lester S. King.

The Life and Works of Eric Gill. 1968.

Reminiscences, by Cecil Gill.

Eric Gill, Typographer, by Beatrice Warde.

Mr. Gill, by David Kindersley.

The Flow of Books and Manuscripts. 1969.

The Case of the "Caxton" Manuscript of Ovid: Reflections on the Legislation Controlling the Export of Works of Art from Great Britain, by A. N. L. Munby.

Every Silver Lining Has a Cloud: The Shaping of the Newberry's Collection, by Lawrence W. Towner.

Some Aspects of Seventeenth-Century Medicine & Science. 1969.

Van Helmont, Boyle, and the Alkahest, by Ladislao Reti.

The Medical Interests of Christopher Wren, by William C. Gibson.

The Terraqueous Globe: The History of Geography and Cartography. 1969.

Edmond Halley and Thematic Geo-Cartography, by Norman J. W. Thrower.

On Chateaubriand's Journey in 1806 from Paris to Jerusalem, by Clarence J. Glacken.

The Task of the Editor. 1969.

The Ideal of Textual Criticism, by James Thorpe.

The Practice of Textual Criticism, by Claude M. Simpson, Jr.

The Lady of Letters in the Eighteenth Century. 1969.

*Letters of Advice to Young Spinsters, by Irvin Ehrenpreis.

*Ladies of Letters in the Eighteenth Century, by Robert Halsband.

The Private Collector and the Support of Scholarship. 1969.

The Book Collector as Public Benefactor, by Louis B. Wright.

The Private Collector and the Literary Scholar, by Gordon N. Ray.

Hobbes and the Epic Tradition of Political Theory, by Sheldon S. Wolin. 1970.

Influences on California Printing. 1970.
The Book Club of California: Its Impress on Fine Printing, by James D. Hart.
The Primavera Press, by Ward Ritchie.
The Primavera Press: A Bibliography, by J. M. Edelstein.

Charles Dickens and George Cruikshank. 1971.
The Fiction of Realism: *Sketches by Boz, Oliver Twist,* and Cruikshank's Illustrations, by J. Hillis Miller.
George Cruikshank: Mirror of an Age, by David Borowitz.

Some Aspects of Eighteenth-Century England. 1971.
Reason and Unreason in the Eighteenth Century: The English Experience, by J. H. Plumb.
A Walk through London with John Gay and A Run with Daniel Defoe, by Vinton A. Dearing.

Congreve Consider'd. 1971.
The "just Decrees of Heav'n" and Congreve's *Mourning Bride,* by Aubrey Williams.
Love, Scandal, and the Moral Milieu of Congreve's Comedies, by Maximillian E. Novak.

Theology in Sixteenth- and Seventeenth-Century England. 1971.
Fast Days and Civil Religion, by Winthrop S. Hudson.
A.D. 1689: The End of the Clerical World, by Leonard J. Trinterud.

English and Continental Views of the Ottoman Empire 1500–1800. 1971.
The Double Veil: Travelers' Views of the Ottoman Empire, Sixteenth through Eighteenth Centuries, by Ezel Kural Shaw.
Sir Paul Rycaut, A Seventeenth-Century Observer of the Ottoman State: Notes for a Study, by C. J. Heywood.
Checklist of Turcica in the Clark Library, compiled by William E. Conway.

Changing Taste in Eighteenth-Century Art and Literature. 1972.
The Art of Piranesi: Looking Backward into the Future, by Robert E. Moore.
"Such, Such Were the Joys": The Boyhood of the Man of Feeling, by Jean H. Hagstrum.

French and English Drama of the Seventeenth Century. 1972.
Tears of Magnanimity in Otway and Racine, by Eugene M. Waith.
From Corneille to Molière: The Metaphor of Value, by Judd D. Hubert.

English Satire. 1972.
  Martin Marprelate: His Identity and Satire, by Leland H. Carlson.
  Satire, and Poetry, and Pope, by Ronald Paulson.
The Editor as Critic and the Critic as Editor. 1973.
  Critical Problems in Editing George Herbert's *The Temple*, by J. Max Patrick.
  A Critic's Apology for Editing Dryden's *The History of the League*, by Alan Roper.
To Tell a Story: Narrative Theory and Practice. 1973.
  Distributing the Middle: Problems of "Movement" in Narrative Poetry, by Earl Miner.
  Mode in Narrative Poetry, by Paul Alpers.
  Sequence and Meaning in Seventeenth-Century Narrative, by Stanley E. Fish.
Theory of the ΛΟΓΟΙ: The Speeches in Classical and Renaissance Narrative, by Richard A. Lanham.
Autobiography, Biography, and the Novel. 1973.
  Seventeenth-Century Autobiography, by William Matthews.
  Defoe, Richardson, Joyce, and the Concept of Form in the Novel, by Ralph W. Rader.
English Portraits of the Seventeenth and Eighteenth Centuries. 1974.
  Pin-ups or Virtues: The Concept of the "Beauties" in Late Stuart Portraiture, by J. Douglas Stewart.
  Portraits of the Author: Lifetime Likenesses of Samuel Johnson, by Herman W. Liebert.
Literature and History. 1974.
  Innovation and Variation: Literary Change and Georgic Poetry, by Ralph Cohen.
  Fiction and Historical Reality: The Hourglass and the Sands of Time, by Murray Kreiger.
The English Legal System: Carryover to the Colonies. 1975.
  The English Criminal Law in Early America, by Joseph H. Smith.
  Law and Liberty (and Order) in Early Massachusetts, by Thomas G. Barnes.
Two English Novelists: Aphra Behn and Anthony Trollope. 1975.
  Aphra Behn's *Oroonoko:* Occasion and Accomplishment, by George Guffey.
  Anthony Trollope as a Reader, by Andrew Wright.

---

*These seminar papers have been collected in a volume edited by Earl Miner and published with the title: *Stuart and Georgian*

Moments: Clark Library Seminar Papers on Seventeenth and Eighteenth Century Literature (University of California Press: $8.50).

The Press has also published two collections of essays presented, outside the seminar series, at the Clark Library:

Illustrious Evidence: Approaches to Early Seventeenth-Century Literature, edited by Earl Miner ($9.50). Contributions by Robert M. Adams, Stanley E. Fish, Frank L. Huntley, Barbara K. Lewalski, Louis L. Martz, and James Thorpe.

England in the Restoration and Early Eighteenth Century: Essays on Culture and Society, edited by H. T. Swedenberg, Jr. ($12.00). Contributions by Robert M. Adams, Bertrand H. Bronson, Jean H. Hagstrum, James W. Johnson, John Loftis, Maximillian E. Novak, the late C. D. O'Malley, James M. Osborn, and Robert R. Wark.